THE POWER OF CONSISTENT SELF-DISCIPLINE

DISCOVER HOW ELITE PERFORMERS USE SELF-CONTROL AND MENTAL TOUGHNESS TO ACHIEVE THEIR GOALS

WILLIAM ANDERSON

CONTENTS

INTRODUCTION

I have not always been a highly disciplined person. I lacked the self-control to stick to a routine when it came to diet or exercise.

I grew up in Romania, an ex-communist country. The revolution took place in 1989 and I was born in 1996 into a country that was already poor. My parents could afford very little while caring for six children on my father's salary. I always dreamed big and wanted to dedicate my life to something meaningful. I wanted to play professional soccer in Europe, but since we didn't have money to send me to a city where I could join a team to fulfill my goal, I was forced to let this dream go.

At age 18, I saw a fitness influencer, who was so dedicated to his elite fitness. I was inspired to become a fitness influencer as well. I said goodbye to Romania and moved to several countries throughout Europe to chase my dreams, all while working up to 12 hours a day. At the same time, I was working out early in the morning, waking up at 3 AM. You can imagine that waking up so early isn't always a sweet thing to do. Looking back, I can tell that self-discipline was one of my best friends. I made all these sacrifices to obtain the PRO CARD in the Men's Physique Division. After several injuries and my body giving up despite my drive, I went back to Romania and, with much hard work, began a business that eventually made a profit.

This success, through all my failures and getting back up, made me realize that my true path led me to write this book to encourage others to never give up on making something meaningful of their goals, of their lives.

Having realized what discipline is and how to use it to improve my life, I want now to pass on what I have learned to you.

Are you someone who wants more out of life? Have you also come to the conclusion that motivation is hard and you cannot count on it? Are you also not sure how to accomplish what you desire? Then, you have come to the right place. You need the core principles that will help you along the way, and this book can offer you that. It will provide you with insights on how to have self-discipline as well as how high performers think and the habits that they have. Furthermore, you will also discover the importance of delayed gratification, the power of focus, the necessity of having an accountability partner, the benefit of visualization, the value of believing in yourself, and more.

In this book, you will also learn how to develop long-term and consistent self-discipline. The goal here is to help you move beyond simply wanting to do better to setting specific goals and achieving them with self-discipline. I also would like to inspire you to act decisively in any activity you decide to pursue.

Why do you need to have consistent self-discipline? There are actually some benefits that you can gain from it, such as having better self-control, understanding the value of time, being more aware of things, having much better judgments, and so forth. Having consistent self-discipline is worth the effort once you can experience all of its benefits. Otherwise, you will only become average and fail to reach your goals for success in life. In addition to learning about the tips to assist you in developing self-discipline, this book will also cover the different ways to have better mental strength. If you struggle to keep moving forward in the face of challenges or if you believe you lack the drive to continue when motivation begins to decline and discomfort sets in, consistent self-discipline is something that you should practice.

Now that you have learned what this book has to offer, it is time for you to get off that couch and start taking action. You should not wait until you have the motivation to do so. This is the first step you can take to achieve consistent self-discipline. Once you can do this, everything else is easy to follow. While you read through this journey to Self-Discipline, use a pencil to make notes or highlight key components that you want to revisit later. If you like to keep your book free of markings use sticky notes or fold the corners of the pages to find notable points later on. If you have the eBook grab a pad or paper and make key notes as you go along.

The power of self-discipline is a journey that begins now. Are you ready? Let's get going!

1

MAKING THINGS AS SIMPLE AS POSSIBLE

"Discipline is doing what you hate to do, but doing it like you love it."- Cus D'Amato

WHAT EXACTLY IS SELF-DISCIPLINE?

Self-discipline is the capability to move forward, , and act despite any physical or mental discomfort (Sasson, 2022). Self-discipline is also generally understood to be conscious control that is directed toward achieving effective results by removing barriers or obstacles (Zimmerman & Kitsantas, 2014). We reveal it when we knowingly opt to work toward wanting to better ourselves in the face of difficult situations like interruptions, challenges, or unfavorable circumstances. Self-discipline is not the same as willpower or self-motivation. Motivation and willpower can lead to it, as well as perseverance, the capacity to carry out our intentions, and also hard work.

For instance, Jane gets up early every morning to work out. She performs very well at her workplace, putting high-value projects first and avoiding distractions in the process. She takes an online class in the evening and receives her master's degree in about a year. This does not seem possible for most people to accomplish. How is it that people like Jane consistently do so much while having the same hours as everyone else? And how will we be able to boast such achievements in both our personal and professional lives like her? The key to this is self-discipline. It is what makes us carry out our great intentions and ambitions, despite our reluctance and unwillingness to take action. If we possess self-discipline, we will be able to postpone momentary pleasure or put up with temporary hardship or discomfort in order to pursue long-term gain in the future.

Self-discipline prevents you from overeating chips or other junk food after deciding to eat healthier meals, or it can prevent you from spending your entire income on useless stuff that you do not need. Every individual has a distinct definition of self-discipline; some of us may find it easier than others to exercise control. Everybody, however, may learn to develop their self-discipline muscles (Parincu, 2022).

Due to the false perception that it is something difficult and that it needs a lot of effort and commitment to get, the term "self-discipline" sometimes elicits some discomfort and reluctance from some people (Parincu, 2022). In reality, developing self-discipline and practicing it can be enjoyable, take little effort, and have significant advantages. As opposed to what some people believe, true self-discipline is not a harsh or strict way of life, and it does not have anything to do with being narrow-minded or having little intellect. This ability is a manifestation of inner courage and perseverance, two qualities that are essential for managing daily activities and accomplishing success.

In the end, we should make self-discipline our best friend. Why? Because we can rely on it as the root of all the good qualities that we dream to possess and the path that will lead us to success, despite all the obstacles on the way.

WHAT ARE THE BENEFITS OF SELF-DISCIPLINE?

Throughout our lives, it is necessary for us to learn and hone the talent of self-discipline since it will benefit us greatly in our lives. There will inevitably be tasks we do not enjoy doing and times when we are distracted from our goals. For this reason, it is crucial to cultivate self-discipline so that we can strive even during these periods of lower motivation. What other benefits does self-discipline have? Here are some of them.

CONTROLLING YOUR EMOTIONS BETTER

Abiding by the morally upright course of action is a small but essential part of discipline. It also becomes one technique for mastering and gaining control over our emotions. With self-discipline, we will be able to keep our worries, hesitations, and all the negativity we have in our heads at bay when faced with a challenging or stressful situation. For example, when doing a team project at work, perhaps you are grouped with a coworker who never does things the right way. You may feel frustrated with them and tempted to get angry instead of trying to teach them how to do things the correct way. In this scenario, you will get exhausted and overwhelmed if you let your emotions take over you. Doing so would be one of the main causes of failure in the many obstacles that life throws our way. Instead of courting failure and then whining about it, we should work on developing self-discipline.

REALIZING THE VALUE OF TIME

Time is a precious resource that waits for no one. Our entire lives, we have been hearing this saying from our elders, whether it was at school or at home. However, did we actually follow it? Each action we take needs to have a timetable. Deciding to adhere to a schedule or, more often than not, deadlines will teach us the value of time in our lives. Eventually, life will be better and more organized when we are disciplined.

HAVING BETTER JUDGMENTS

Decision-making is one of the most powerful abilities that we, humans, have been given, with profound implications for our lives, and not only. Thus, we can either make a wise decision and choose to live today and tomorrow better, or we can choose badly and fall into a deep pit hole. We can better distinguish between what is good and what violates the laws of nature and society when we have self-discipline. For example, when we realize that we are really intoxicated, we can decide whether to take a taxi or drive ourselves home. That one decision has the potential to change everything.

MAKING YOU BECOME MORE ACTIVE

We will begin to understand that life is not about sitting around waiting for a chance to knock at your door if we practice self-discipline. Our minds gradually come to the realization that sitting around and moping will not help us in the long run. At that point, we start acting and taking control of our lives. In turn, as we let go of the laziness that had been preventing us for so long from taking a step toward our desire, we will be able to become a better and improved version of ourselves.

BECOMING MORE SELF-AWARE

When we develop the ability to be self-disciplined, we learn more about ourselves and our capabilities. We have the opportunity to recognize our strengths and shortcomings as well as work on them according to our needs and circumstances. That makes it possible for us to get rid of the personality traits that have prevented us from succeeding in life. After a while, we will be able to stop relying on our friends or even our families to judge us more positively. We will become our own best critics.

GROWING INTO YOUR BEST SELF

Only when we deserve it does success come to us. With our present personalities, we may not be able to become successful in life. We must therefore make changes day after day and strive to be our best selves. We can constantly better ourselves through self-discipline. When we regularly practice something, we get better and better each day. Thus, self-discipline is essential for achievement and personal development in life.

IMPROVING YOUR PERFORMANCE

If we want to improve in our careers, it is absolutely essential that we are driven and fully committed to our work regardless of how large or pointless the task appears to be. We need commitment anywhere, whether we are hosting a friend's birthday party or giving a presentation. Both on a professional and a personal level, taking things lightly can turn out to be very disastrous. Of course, no host wants to hear negative comments about the party they have organized. Also, no one would want to give a bad presentation and get humiliated in front of the audience as this can be very shameful. In all areas of our lives, we must be dedicated and motivated. That is one of the major points supporting the value of discipline since it teaches us how to perform better.

IMPROVING YOUR PERSONAL RELATIONSHIPS

Tom decided to procrastinate working on his project during the week because he felt lazy and unmotivated to do so. When the weekend arrived, he realized that he needed to finish the project by the next Monday. Instead of using his weekend off for spending time with his wife and kids, he had to work on completing the project. In this case, Tom did not practice self-discipline when he actually needed to. When we have self-discipline, we always finish our work on time. There is a ton of time available to us. Because of this, we will be able to have all the available time to bond with our loved ones. We can use our time without worrying about unfinished business. A time spent together without guilt—this is a result of having a strong self-discipline. In the end, all of our personal relationships will be improved significantly.

IS DISCIPLINE SOMETHING YOU INHERIT?

Discipline comes from inside of us. Interestingly, it does not really matter if we come from a family that consistently exercises discipline because it is neither contagious nor inherited. We must develop discipline ourselves; it cannot come from outside of us. For instance, the majority of us have encountered people who have come from dysfunctional families, unfortunate life situations, and every imaginable terrible circumstance, yet these people are disciplined.

We do not get discipline from our families. Some people are very disciplined and were born into dysfunctional families; others are not very self-disciplined and were born into very good families. As an example, people from problematic family circumstances typically follow one of two ways. They either let themselves dwell on their pain and, sadly, never reach their full potential, or they embrace their struggles to motivate them to rise above their difficulties and improve themselves for the better. Which direction they take is entirely up to each of them to decide. They simply need the strength of character to avoid repeating the mistakes that made their family lives hard once they are adults and have separated from their families. We can decide to act differently if we recognize the areas where our parents failed. For instance, a parent who has a gambling addiction that causes their entire family agony can teach their kids the behavior they need to avoid to stop the cycle.

This indicates that nobody can point the finger at someone else for their lack of discipline. We have no right to hold our friends, parents, or even our schools accountable for our own lack of control. We must own up to it. We need to be able to motivate ourselves. Nobody else can give us the self-discipline, emotional restraint, and control we need to succeed in our lives. Every person must choose for themselves, understanding that effective discipline is quite difficult, particularly when first starting.

IS DISCIPLINE YOUR CHOICE TO MAKE?

Nobody just gets up from their sleep one day and declares that they have mastered the art of self-discipline so suddenly. Similar to a muscle, discipline needs to be developed over time. Have you tried to train your self-discipline today? Perhaps your answer to this is no. However, you might have already made a few choices this morning that would make you say yes to the question. The issue here is that we frequently pay more attention to the aspects of life where discipline is lacking than to those where it is developed well.

People who are excellent at exercising self-discipline do so frequently because they consistently take the appropriate actions to tackle the problem at hand. It means that discipline is a choice that we decide to take in order to overcome the challenges we have to face. Over time, maintaining a particular behavior becomes a habit. For instance, even though you enjoy sleeping, you only sleep a maximum of six hours per night. You value your love for your family and your ability to contribute at work more than sleep. You simply care for other aspects of your life more than sleep, not because you dislike sleep any less. In this scenario, you choose to prioritize your loved ones, your job, and your family over getting more sleep.

We will be able to sustain our efforts and take the steps required for achievement by choosing to adopt discipline in our lives. Without self-discipline, we are bound to act hastily and recklessly. We can put ourselves in check by leading a disciplined life, and it is entirely our decision to choose whether we want to have self-discipline or not.

KEY TAKEAWAYS

- As explained above, self-discipline is the capability to move forward, maintain motivation, and act despite any physical or mental discomfort. It is the path we must take in order to accomplish success.
- It also has a lot of advantages for us such as controlling our emotions better, realizing the value of time, having better judgments, making us more active, becoming more aware, supporting us to become the best version of ourselves, improving our performance, and making our personal relationships better.
- Discipline is also not something that we inherit from other people because it comes from within ourselves.

2

HOW TO INSTILL A DESIRE FOR CONSISTENT SELF-DISCIPLINE

"You don't get discipline from an external source. You have to get it from you."- Jocko Willink

The key to being able to lead others and also ourselves is discipline. Focus and self-control lead to contentment, happiness, and success. When we exercise self-control and discipline, we can achieve more of the goals that are most important to us. Self-discipline is the bridge between setting goals and realizing them. However, it is not that easy to get the desire to actually have consistent self-discipline in our lives. How do we do this? What are the steps we can take to accomplish it?

ENVISIONING THE FUTURE

IMAGINING YOUR IDEAL SELF

The first step to getting the desire for self-discipline is to imagine what your ideal self would be. This is the best and highest version of yourself that you can think of. With this in mind, consider the following questions:

- Who do you hope to become?
- What do you hope to do, encounter, and possess?
- What kind of life do you desire to have in the future?
- What contributions, whether small or significant, do you intend to make to the world?

- What type of work will suit your ideal self?
- What kind of life would you lead if you succeeded in becoming your ideal self? What drives your desire to adopt this identity? Why do you choose it?

Write your responses to these questions. When you are through, you will have clearly defined your ideal self. You now have something to work toward. A lot of us are scared of what our ideal selves are like because we fear that we will never be able to become them. However, if we refuse to imagine and think of it, how would we ever accomplish it? We need to envision the best version of ourselves before we can take all the other necessary steps to reach that point.

WRITING DOWN AND VISUALIZING THE ACTIONS AND BEHAVIORS ATTACHED TO THIS IDEAL VERSION OF YOURSELF

What habits must you form in order to live up to your ideal self and potential? What actions will you take to accomplish that? What behaviors do you need to adopt for that? Here are some of the forms that discipline may take:

- Health and fitness: Perhaps you can make a timetable to work out at the gym three times a week and follow through with the schedule as best as you are able to.
- Mental and intellectual: You can decide to read one book a week or write down a short story or poem when you have time on the weekends in order to train your intellect and brain.
- Social and emotional: You may choose to spend more quality time with your family or partner by planning a weekly date night or family dinner at a restaurant to bond more with them.

- Spiritual and religious: You can make a schedule to meditate for 15 minutes every day or go to church every week in order to deepen your spirituality.

When we can visualize all these types of discipline that we wish to apply in our lives, it will be much easier for us to do them. If we know what is waiting for us in the future, we will feel more inspired and motivated to start taking action to have consistent self-discipline.

THINKING ABOUT THE END RESULTS

Developing a vision of the outcomes and hanging onto it is key to the self-discipline battle. One little, wise choice keeps self-discipline in place when we are presented with a challenge that slows us down or completely breaks us away from the path. Instead of surrendering to temptation and the pressure of the present, we need to be able to think forward. We can overcome the challenge by learning to say no to the temptations that come our way. When we can envision the end results of self-discipline that are possible, we will be able to apply it in our lives more easily and with fewer struggles.

RECOGNIZING THE REASONS FOR LACK OF DISCIPLINE

There are several things that influence our success. All kinds of abilities, habits, and mindsets play a big role in our own achievements. Although there are other important factors, self-discipline stands out among the rest. When we lack self-discipline, we might lead a lifestyle that is unhealthy.

Our capacity for self-discipline is one of the most important factors in determining our level of success in life. Its effects can be observed in a variety of life aspects. It bears repeating: If we desire to achieve our goals and live a happy life, we need to have consistent self-discipline. Yet a lot of us often lack this. Why does this happen? What are the reasons?

MISUNDERSTANDING THE BASIC CONCEPT

Many people struggle with self-discipline mostly because they misunderstand what this concept implies. From their perspective, self-discipline is something uncomfortable and obsessive. They wished that discipline was easy and fun to do. Because of this, whenever these people attempt to become more disciplined, it ends up being a struggle that does not feel fair to them. Because they do not like it, they quickly go back to their usual habits.

BEING LAZY

If we have a hard time practicing self-discipline, it may be because we lack inner strength and are too lazy. In this case, we avoid engaging in things that need persistence and effort. It is in our human nature that we prefer peaceful, enjoyable behaviors to demanding tasks that need a lot of effort. In contrast to self-discipline, laziness is comfortable and not complicated. It is much easier to sit around and live in our comfort zone instead of taking action to apply self-discipline in our lives. A lot of us fall into this and have a lack of discipline.

FALLING INTO LIFE TEMPTATIONS

Almost all of us are very vulnerable to many temptations day after day. Social media and TV advertising constantly scream at us to buy their products. Supermarkets and shopping centers offer a wide range of goods for sale. We also have access to a number of entertainment options, from social media, TV shows, and movies to nice restaurants, music concerts, and many other distractions in this modern world. They all seem so impossible to escape from. How can we refuse to browse through social media that offers a pleasant escape from everyday life or avoid the beautifully displayed and tempting items in the store? Self-discipline is bound to be lacking if all of these pleasures are accepted and followed carelessly and without using common sense.

BEING SCARED TO FAIL

We all fear something. Another reason for a lack of self-discipline is when we have a fear of failure. This speaks to a deficiency of inner strength, suppressing initiative and determination. Oftentimes accepting failure results in losing control. When people can accept the potential of failing, it will be challenging to maintain self-discipline. Before something even happens, those who have a fear of failure will be pessimistic from the start, and they might even decide to not take action at all, fearing the end results.

UNDERSTANDING THE CONSEQUENCES OF LACK OF DISCIPLINE

Everybody can recall a period when they procrastinated in moving toward their goals. We desire to eat healthier, yet we find it impossible to give up the sweet treats we enjoy. Despite our intention to get out of bed sooner, we often stay up late, until after one in the morning. We all have been there before. If we continue to practice the one negative habit that prevents us from mastering the main habit that will ultimately lead to our achievements, we will feel terrible.

In the same way that discipline has its advantages, it can also have negative consequences. As an example, we may frequently find ourselves hitting the snooze button after knowing that we have made the commitment to get up at 6 a.m. in the morning. The negative consequence of this is that we would not get things done, and we would end up getting angry at ourselves for not being further ahead on a specific task that we wished to have completed by a certain time. In addition to getting angry, there are several more consequences of our lack of discipline that we should be aware of.

PREVENTING YOU FROM ACCOMPLISHING YOUR GOALS

Distractions can also increase in this area. If we are not careful, accepting even little distractions because of our own excuses will keep us frustrated and pull us further away from our goals and purpose. When we do not wish to do something, many of us will create different excuses so that we can avoid doing it. After that, we will regret it. We would ask ourselves why we do not get things done and become irritated because we have not seen the progress we hope to make.

LOWERING YOUR SELF-ESTEEM

In your mind, this may seem stupid, but give it some thought. Because you lack something or you have someone that you are envious of, you experience poor self-esteem or insecurity. When we see how easy it is for certain people to work or run their businesses, and they are making a lot of money, while we are still trying to be stable enough, it will make us feel like we should just quit what we are doing since we are nowhere close to where we need to be. Our self-esteem level will decrease when we do not have self-discipline because our progress is hindered by our own inaction.

TAKING AWAY YOUR FOCUS

A messy surrounding leads to a cluttered mind, which will take away our focus from our tasks. If everything around us is disorganized, then our thoughts will also be disorganized. When our spaces are not arranged well, we will not be able to take action to transform ourselves. We need to have a strategy for this, and self-discipline will keep us moving forward with our intended course of action. If we cannot practice self-discipline, we will stray away from our focus and not follow through with our plans.

SHOWING THAT YOU LACK SELF-RESPECT

When we are not sure or do not know how to do something, we will give up on it. We neglect the fact that we are also making the decision to break our commitment. We all enjoy being lazy and not doing anything, but we do not like it when we are disrespected. This kind of lack of discipline is dangerous because when we decide to abandon a task, we disrespect ourselves and our own commitment.

MAKING YOU PROCRASTINATE MORE

If we lack self-discipline, laziness will cause us to put things off more. We will not be able to accomplish our goals if we do this. When we do not know how to control ourselves and fall into temptations, we will procrastinate on our tasks and produce poor-quality work in the end.

KEY TAKEAWAYS

- Before we can start on our journey to have consistent self-discipline, we need to first find the desire and willpower to begin it.
- In order to discover this desire, we have to imagine our ideal selves, write down and visualize the actions and behaviors attached to the ideal version of ourselves, and what kind of outcomes will come our way from having consistent self-discipline.
- We also need to realize that there are reasons that can cause us to have a lack of discipline, such as having a misunderstanding of the basic concept, being lazy or lacking inner power, falling into life temptations, and being scared to fail.
- If we fail to improve our self-discipline, there are consequences that we must face. It will prevent us from achieving our goals, lower our self-esteem, take away our focus, show that we do not have respect for ourselves, and make us procrastinate more.
- Once we realize all of the above, we will be able to see how important it is to have self-discipline and that we need to start applying it consistently in our lives so that we can stay on the path to success.

3

GOAL-SETTING AND SELF-DISCIPLINE

"When you have a goal, when you have a vision, everything becomes easy."- Arnold Schwarzenegger

Of all the factors that influence someone's success and happiness, only one ensures long-term, sustained success in all areas of life, and that is self-discipline. For instance, developing self-discipline can be difficult, but it will be well worth the effort in the field of health and fitness. Many of us may feel insecure about how our bodies look after eating so much junk food all the time. We want to lose weight in order to feel better, look better, and wear all the clothes we want. In order to achieve this,

29

we need to set specific goals, such as planning to go to the gym three times a week or starting a healthy meal plan by cooking homemade food. As a result of being disciplined in this area, we will develop a better, healthier lifestyle and become more confident about how we look. That is why we need to set goals before we can have consistent self-discipline. Those who do not have a clear and specific goal in life will find it more challenging to maintain discipline since they are still not sure what they desire to achieve. By contrast, we are far more inclined to possess the willpower to chase our goals if we have a certain purpose that we wish to see come true in the future.

WHY SHOULD YOU SET SPECIFIC GOALS?

Do you have any personal goals? What are your plans for the upcoming year? What do you want out of life? Creating goals is the very first step in achieving them. It represents the beginning of our achievements. It occurs when we start actively shaping our lives rather than just passively existing for no reason at all. We must establish our precise goals in order to help us develop consistent self-discipline. If we do not have specific goals, we may not be able to have self-discipline because we are not sure what we want to achieve from it. Before we learn about the steps in setting goals, let us consider the advantages we can get from them.

HAVING MORE CONTROL OF YOUR LIFE

These days, a lot of people are living their lives as if they are sleeping. Despite their best efforts, they do not feel as though they are making progress toward their goals. This is a result of their lack of direction over their goals and where they wish to go in the future. Adults who have worked for years are surprised when they approach their 30s or 40s, and students are unsure of what to do next after graduating from college (Celes, 2022). Without setting goals, we might end up spending our entire lives bouncing up and down without accomplishing anything. We are really just achieving other people's objectives, not our own. We will begin living a life that we have intentionally created when we take the time to set goals and consider our ambitions and aspirations. We should actively take charge and consider what we want for ourselves as opposed to having others tell us what to do and which direction to take.

ACQUIRING MAXIMUM RESULTS

All accomplished people, professional athletes, and top performers set their own goals. We all have heard of Mark Zuckerberg, a self-taught computer programmer as well as the co-founder, chairman, and CEO of Meta (META), previously recognized as Facebook. He is known for creating the social networking site in his dormitory at Harvard University in 2004, while it was still called Facemash, along with some of his friends (Downey, 2019). Before deciding to create the site, he had set goals and even gone on to make it in his dorm room. Although not having all the fancy facilities, Zuckerberg was able to realize his goal because of how disciplined he was.

When we set goals, we have something to aim for. Instead of sitting back and waiting for everything to happen by itself, we need to make sure that we are challenging ourselves to achieve the best results. We also need to realize that there is also room for improvement. How will things go better if we do not set clear goals and benchmarks? There is essentially nothing to work toward, and although we might be devoting a lot of effort, it may not be effective. When we decide to set goals, we are shooting for the moon. We take action more than we otherwise would because of the goals we set.

What do you hope to achieve in a year? How about in three years? Setting goals forces us to prepare ahead, which allows us to develop an action plan. Even if things do not go exactly as we had planned, it is still okay because we can review, modify our plans, and then guide our lives in the direction of our goals slowly but surely.

GIVING YOU CLEAR FOCUS

By setting goals, we will be able to become more focused. Our goals offer us a clear focus on what to concentrate our time and energy on, whereas our life purpose provides us with a general direction. Let's imagine that you have decided to start a bakery. Even though you do not know how to make it happen, just establishing a goal provides you with something to focus on. As you come up with ideas, you realize that you may begin this goal by researching the brands and local bakery market. You will try to understand people's preferences for desserts and bread. After that, you can enroll in baking classes to develop your abilities. You may then test recipes and serve your products to friends before selling them at the same time. We can think of the outcomes as the output and our energy as the input. When we have a goal, we establish a focus point in which we are able to direct our energy to gain the maximum benefit.

CREATING ACCOUNTABILITY

Setting goals will make us become accountable. Instead of only talking, we are now obligated to take action. This accountability is one that you have to yourself and not to everyone else. Nobody knows and is aware of all the goals we set. Even when we succeed in reaching our goals, others have nothing to benefit from it. By having clear goals, we can know if we are on track, and if not, we will be able to determine how to solve them.

As an example, if you want to establish your own personal blog, you need to set goals, like finishing a specific number of posts per week, reaching a target traffic goal each week, and acquiring a particular number of clients each month. This will make you accountable for achieving these goals. You will then need to keep an eye on your progress weekly while working on your plan. You also have to make the appropriate adjustments if you ever realize you are falling short.

LIVING YOUR BEST LIFE

Goals also guarantee that we get the most out of life. Time will go by in our lives whether we like it or not. We will be a year older in a year. We will be ten years older in ten years. Setting goals with clear deadlines and measurements helps us make the most of our time here in this world. Our goals will enable us to maximize our life purpose if we have already found it.

Let's imagine the world as our oyster. There are countless possibilities for activities, adventures, and interactions with people that we can have. There are endless opportunities for what we are able to achieve. What if you had complete freedom? What would you like to see, do, and encounter in life? We must set our goals, work toward them, and observe them as we build our lives for the better.

HOW DO YOU SET YOUR GOALS?

Setting goals is a useful strategy for developing consistent self-discipline. We can choose how to use our time and resources to achieve maximum outcomes by setting goals and establishing a clear plan for how we will get to our desired targets. Without goals, it might be challenging to plan how to advance toward becoming self-disciplined and having a successful life. How do we set goals then? Here are some ways we can use it.

VISUALIZING YOUR GOALS AND EXPERIENCING THEM

If our goal is to spend more time with our family by not working nights and weekends, we must experience the goal by visualizing it or by really doing it right away. This will strengthen our self-discipline as we proceed through the necessary measures to accomplish the goal. It is also crucial to keep ourselves healthy physically, mentally, emotionally, as well as spiritually. It takes more than simply having enough money to avoid working outside the home to be able to spend more time with our family. We also need to be physically healthy, capable of handling stress, and willing to invest time in our own personal growth.

PLANNING AHEAD

Some external influences will always present a challenge to our daily routines. Making strategies for the best, worst, and most likely scenarios will help us keep our routines. For example, we can go on a vacation in order to find situations that can challenge our self-discipline (Ali, 2021). Self-disciplined people will use their vacation time and actively build flexibility into their daily schedule instead of sticking to a strict schedule that will never work. When returning to a normal schedule, it is much easier to make adjustments because they already know what needs to change.

UNDERSTANDING YOUR WHY

This is possibly the most important technique for developing strong self-discipline. We can concentrate better on the bigger picture if we are aware of why we want to accomplish a certain goal. Knowing why we desire to lose weight, such as to reduce our chance of developing diabetes and its complications, will increase our likelihood of success. Simply wishing to lose weight because we think we would be healthier at a lighter weight is far less likely to be successful. We can take it a step further by considering how diabetes affects not just us but also our family and the whole population. It is much more challenging to run a marathon just to reach the finish line than it is to run a marathon in support of a purpose or charity that is precious to our hearts.

SETTING SMART GOALS

SMART is an abbreviation that stands for specific, measurable, achievable, relevant, and time-based (Herrity, 2022). Every component of the SMART system functions in harmony to provide a goal that is thoroughly planned out, identifiable, and trackable. A lot of us may have previously set goals that were challenging to accomplish because they were framed incorrectly, excessively, or insufficiently. A badly constructed goal might make achieving it seem overwhelming and impossible. These issues can be resolved by setting SMART goals. Whether we are making goals for our personal or professional lives, employing the SMART goal structure may give us a strong framework for success.

- Specific: We need to be as detailed and precise as we can about what we wish to accomplish. We will discover the actions required to attain our goals more thoroughly the more specific our goals are (Herrity, 2022). We can say, for example, "I want to get a job managing an HR team for a startup company."
- Measurable: What concrete evidence will demonstrate that we are moving closer to our goal? If our goal is to manage an HR team for a startup company, for instance, we can measure our progress by the number of HR roles we have applied for or the number of interviews we have had. Setting checkpoints along the journey will allow us to assess

our progress and make necessary adjustments. When we reach these checkpoints, we need to remember to reward ourselves in a small yet meaningful way.

- Achievable: Have you established achievable goals? We will be able to stay motivated and focused if we set goals we can practically achieve within a set period of time. Using the above case of getting a job managing an HR team, we should be aware of the qualifications, experience, and abilities required to obtain that position. We have to consider whether we can attain a goal now or whether we need to take more preparation steps to be properly ready before we start working toward it (Herrity, 2022).

- Relevant: We need to think about if our goals are relevant when setting them. Our goals should all be consistent with our values and longer-term objectives. We may want to reconsider a goal if it does not help us achieve our broader ambitions. We should question why the objective is significant to us, how reaching it will benefit us, and how it will advance our long-term objectives.

- Time-based: What time frame do you have in mind for your goal? A deadline can help motivate us and assist us with prioritizing. For instance, we can allow ourselves six months if our goal is to obtain a promotion to a higher-ranking senior position. By then, if we have not succeeded in our goal, give it some thought and consider the reason why. It is possible that our goal was unachievable, our schedule was too tight, or we encountered unforeseen obstacles.

KEY TAKEAWAYS

- Consistent self-discipline starts with goal-setting. If we do not have a specific goal, with precise or clear reasons for wanting to attain that goal, the likelihood of us being disciplined will be very low.
- Setting goals will give you a clear focus and more control over your life, and encourage you to be more accountable, while also allowing you to get maximum results and envision your best life.
- Setting SMART goals goes hand in hand with visualizing, planning, and understanding the reasons for them. To achieve our goal, we need to establish a plan and, no matter what obstacles stand in our way, we have to remain dedicated to doing whatever is necessary to accomplish it.

4

DOING SOMETHING THAT SUCKS EVERYDAY

"Do something that sucks every single day of your life. That's how you grow."- David Goggins

Why should we do something that sucks? This is a challenge that encourages us to recognize and build on our abilities, even as we recognize our limits. It concentrates and capitalizes on our biggest potential, which lies in our top strengths and skills. However, to make that potential a reality and thus perform at our best requires self-discipline.

Everything worth accomplishing needs sacrifice at the start. Confidence is developed through success, and in order to succeed, we must do things that suck, are difficult, and are uncomfortable. Even when we think that we have finished a task, we are actually just 40% done (Davy, 2019). The Navy SEALs refer to this as the 40% rule, which was made popular by David Goggins, who competed in 14 track races totaling more than 100 miles each while spending most of his time serving on active duty and with a possibly deadly heart condition that only allowed him to function with around 75% of his heart's capacity (Firsich, 2020).

David Goggins encouraged us to ignore our strengths and concentrate on our shortcomings because they challenge and unsettle us, and we should get used to feeling uncomfortable. Real improvement comes from a willingness to experience discomfort by confronting our inner monsters, fears, and negative emotions. Once we embrace the challenge, though, how do we go about doing things that suck and are uncomfortable?

FACING THINGS THAT SUCK

How frequently did you have a challenging task to complete? And how often have you simply avoided dealing with it? We have all come across this situation. When we deal with it and get it done, it usually is not as horrible as we initially feared. The truth is, we only need to face it first, and everything will become easier. For example, James has been wanting to resume his fitness routine. He usually likes to run, lift weights, do yoga, and practice martial arts. Anything further is an additional advantage for him. The challenge here is integrating it into his family life. He had to accept the idea that in order to run and lift weights, he would need to wake up early and make it a priority. He, therefore, has developed this habit for over four weeks. When his alarm goes off at 5:30 a.m., he starts getting ready for his run. We all know that running so early in the morning sucks; it still annoys James even after four whole weeks.

But there is another way to look at what sucks, and that is to see it as a character-building activity. No matter how hard it is in the beginning, we feel good afterward. It feels amazing to do something that we do not look forward to or are unsure we can complete. Additionally, it raises the bar for what we believe we are capable of. Thus, by starting the day with an activity that we dread, everything else that day will be a little bit easier. Pushing through one challenging situation puts the upcoming ones into perspective. We develop tolerance to things that suck. Moreover, it cultivates strength, persistence, and a fighting spirit.

For instance, your supervisor criticizes you, you then have a horrible argument with your coworker at work, and you make an error in your big daily tasks. These will still be annoying and upsetting. However, when you have already overcome a challenge that morning, they do not have as big of a negative impact on you anymore.

GETTING YOURSELF READY

If we decide to do something that sucks, we will encounter internal resistance initially. We can, however, take action to lessen the resistance. If we want to run at 6 a.m. each morning, the time and run do not change. However, there are other things we are able to change. If we plan to run, we need to do certain things to prepare for the night beforehand. Perhaps we can lay out our freshly washed shorts, shirts, and socks and put them on the couch. We can also prepare our jogging clothes and sneakers and put them in a place that we can view. We may also place our headphones and smartphones on the table next to our clothing.

Moreover, if we find it hard to change in the bedroom because we are afraid to wake up our partner, we can go out of the room, turn on the bathroom light, and get dressed there instead. As we have prepared our headphones for the run, we can put on music that will be able to motivate us. Because we have found the motivation and gotten relaxed, it is then easier for us to stretch and walk prior to beginning the run. All these preparations are the things that we can do in order to run early in the morning even though it is very difficult.

UNDERSTANDING THE EXPOSURE THEORY

Using the example above, we want to start waking up early to run and get a good fitness routine. We need to keep in mind that we plan to get up at 6 a.m. in the morning. We have to know that we will not break any world record on our first day of doing that. We should give our bodies time to warm up and get used to it. This is where our minds get in the zone. As time goes by, we can then start to put in more effort and increase the challenge as well as intensity. The idea behind this also drives exposure therapy.

When something or someone makes people uncomfortable or afraid, they are more likely to avoid it. Therapists implement the concept of exposure therapy to help patients in overcoming their fears and anxieties by breaking down the cycle of avoidance and anxiety (Yetman, 2021). It works out by presenting someone with a fear-inducing stimulus in a safe setting. A person with social anxiety, for instance, might avoid coming to events or busy places.

In order to make the patient feel at ease in these kinds of social situations, a therapist will expose the patient to them in exposure therapy. They must learn to be comfortable with any level of stimulation they need to handle (Yetman, 2021).

As another example, the majority of people's greatest fear is public speaking. In order to face this by using exposure theory, we can get a person to talk face-to-face with another person. Then, we can encourage them to talk to two people at once. Afterward, we can ask them to speak to three people. They can continue doing this until 100 people are in the room. By increasing the stimulus, we also increase our capacity for dealing with it. We greatly enhance resilience in this case.

We can do this too with anything that sucks. We can start off slowly and gradually increase our effort and stimulus as time passes. After that, we will see that we have transformed ourselves. We learn how to handle situations that really suck, including things that we previously never thought of doing or completing.

KEY TAKEAWAYS

- When we do something that sucks, we will change. We will develop previously lacking confidence, persistence, and thus self-discipline.
- If we plan to do things that suck, we need to do them first thing in the morning. Afterward, everything will become easier to do.
- Once we can overcome things that suck, we will never forget the feeling of strength, accomplishment, and satisfaction.
- When we do things that suck, we can begin slowly and then steadily increase our effort and intensity. After that, we will be able to significantly increase our adaptability and see how much we can change.

5

CHANGING WHAT YOU CAN CHANGE AND LETTING GO OF WHAT YOU CANNOT CHANGE

"If you can't control it, let it go."- Gary R. McClain

When something does not go our way, it is quite easy to start thinking of the wrong things. We stray into areas and thoughts over which we have no control. We begin to dwell on all the negative aspects of our situation and worry about all the negative outcomes that might occur. We lose sight of our role in determining our reality, which clouds our judgment. We make an effort to remain optimistic and efficient on good days. On bad days, we drown in worry over imagining what the future will hold. We picture it, then begin to experience it, leaving us feeling powerless and afraid. When we focus on what we cannot change, we stop doing things we are supposed to do to become disciplined in order to reach success.

The key is to channel our efforts into the things we can control, letting go of the rest. By doing so, we can increase our resilience and begin to make progress regardless of the level of chaos going on around us. Attempting to control everything in life is a losing battle. Despite our best efforts, focusing on things whose outcomes we cannot actually change is a waste of energy. The first step to this is to recognize what we can and cannot control.

HOW DO YOU FEEL MORE IN CONTROL?

Focusing on what we can change about ourselves or our surroundings and trying to move in the right direction will help us feel more in control. We will be able to greatly improve our quality of life if we take charge of everything within our power and let go of the rest. The first step in empowering ourselves is recognizing what we can and cannot control and then redirecting our energy to those things. We can fully accept responsibility for our lives in this manner, without adding to our stress levels in the process. It all begins with us; an aspect of leading a self-disciplined and healthy life entails taking complete accountability for our actions and what we are able to control in our lives.

So how do we regain control of the things that are within our reach? The answer lies in practicing mindfulness, which involves being attentive, self-aware, and involved in what we are doing and where we are at that present (Bastos, 2020). When we practice mindfulness, we develop the attentional skill of 'seeing' our thoughts and feelings and changing how we respond to them (Christian, 2021). We can gradually teach ourselves to focus on the here and now in order to be more aware of our thoughts and reactions to the environment around us.

In order to have better self-discipline, we need the transformational power of mindfulness that is accessible to everyone. Here are some methods to help us begin our journey toward getting control over what we can control.

PAYING CLOSE ATTENTION TO YOUR FEELINGS AND EMOTIONS

We are encouraged to get rid of the notion that we have any control over our feelings and emotions through the practice of mindfulness. Alternatively, it encourages us to pay more attention to what we are feeling and thus understand it better. We can better control the influence that emotions have on our behavior by becoming aware of the ups and downs of our own thoughts. In this sense, mindfulness is a method of control. As we become more conscious of our emotions and how we react to them, we will understand that the voices in our heads are not always to be trusted. Getting control over how feelings and emotions might affect our behavior requires acknowledging that occasionally our thoughts are not helpful and they do not have to be the ones that should determine what we do.

CONCENTRATING ON THE PRESENT

We are able to access mindfulness at any time and from any place. An important technique for developing a mindful state is to keep our focus on the present moment. Since tranquility and peace of mind are much more likely to be found in the present, it is important to keep our minds in there. That is also the place where our focus is strongest and in which we can be far more in tune with our feelings, thoughts, and physical sensations (Bastos, 2020). In contrast, when our attention is on another point in time, emotions and feelings that are still present in the past or the future might not only cause us to get distracted, but they can also develop as disorders like anxiety and depression.

When our focus and attention are on the present, we are not preoccupied with what may have been or the things that might happen later. That is, we view our feelings and emotions as temporary instead of permanent. We can refocus our attention when we realize that we are becoming bogged down in negative feelings and emotions by being mindful of the present. This allows us to take charge and be in control of how our emotions affect us.

TAKING ACTION TO CREATE CHANGE

It takes practice to become aware of our emotions and feelings as well as to teach our minds to concentrate on the present. However, the more we do it, the better we will get, and the outcome can significantly affect our well-being in a positive way. We can start doing this by setting some achievable goals. A great approach to getting motivated to take action and make great changes is to think about where we wish our lives to go and the kind of person we desire to become in the future.

WHAT ARE THE THINGS YOU CAN CONTROL IN LIFE?

The main idea of this chapter is to concentrate on the things we can control in order to have consistent self-discipline, but before that, we need to know what those things are first. Here are a few aspects of our lives that we have control over. We will be amazed by the improvements that can develop over time when we can make small progress in these aspects.

HOW YOU COMMUNICATE WITH YOUR LOVED ONES

Although they are not always simple and easy, relationships are the basis of a pleasant and healthy life. Even though we have no control over the actions of our loved ones, we do have power over how we act in a relationship. Healthy communication is where it all begins. Words frequently fall short when trying to convey abstract feelings and thinking processes. In this case, we can use an assertive communication style, which is fantastic news. Developing an assertive communication style can help us get our point across, prevent misunderstandings, and gain a deeper understanding of how our loved ones are feeling (Christian, 2021).

In a relationship, the only one we are able to control is ourselves. If we want to communicate in a healthy way with our loved ones, the following are some examples of an assertive communication style:

- Making direct eye contact. This demonstrates the speaker's self-confidence
- Having an assertive posture that strikes the balance between seriousness and casualness. For instance, rigid posture may be interpreted as hostile, while slouching may be interpreted as weak (Lonczak, 2020).
- Showing the right facial expressions. For the proper message to be sent, expressions that are calm and relaxed are necessary to use.
- Using the right tone of voice. A strong voice indicates assertiveness, whereas raising your voice displays and will probably invite hostility.

HOW YOU MAINTAIN YOUR MENTAL HEALTH

Mental and physical wellness are equally important. Our quality of life is greatly influenced by how actively we take care of our psychological, emotional, and social well-being. Interacting with others, getting sufficient sleep, exercising regularly, and seeking professional assistance when necessary are all ways to maintain good mental health. If life seems out of control, it is extremely crucial to take care of our mental health. When our minds are healthy, and we stay away from bad thoughts, it will be much easier for us to do all the things we need to do. We will not miss all the important things in life when we keep our mental health in check at all times.

HOW YOU RESPOND WHEN SOMETHING NEGATIVE HAPPENS

Our ability to make decisions is at its worst when powerful emotions like fear, rage, or envy take control. It is very easy to lose control and act rashly in this kind of situation. Learning to manage our reactions entails learning to regulate our emotions. By moving from a position of reaction to a place of response, we can do just that. Reacting is defined as acting hastily and unconsciously in response to our feelings. Responding entails pausing to consider what we are thinking or feeling. Prior to engaging in a disagreement or making a choice based on fear, we must ask for the time and space that we require to understand the situation. We can return to the issue once we have calmed down in a more fresh, problem-solving state of mind.

WHAT YOU DO WITH YOUR FREE TIME

We can choose how we use our spare time even though we cannot always control how much of it we have. Our lives can be significantly affected by how we spend our free time. Here are a handful of the activities successful people engage in during their free time, as reported by Inc (Demers, 2022):

- Reading helps us learn new concepts, expand our vocabulary, and preserve our cognitive function.
- Taking courses strengthens our portfolio and makes us more attractive to employers.
- Volunteering helps us gain perspective on life, contribute to our local community, and find our purpose in this world.
- Networking opens up different prospects for both our personal and professional lives.
- Working out can benefit both our physical and mental health.
- Spending quality time with our loved ones fosters connection and creates a network of support.
- Hobbies help us stay creative and mentally active.

WHAT KIND OF NEWS YOU WATCH

A balanced diet is about more than just providing our bodies with healthy foods. It also extends to those things intended for our intellectual consumption, or even for mere entertainment. Our mental well-being is harmed by excessive exposure to negative social media or news reports (Davey, 2020). Although we have no control over the crises that arise in the world, we do have power over how much news we consume, the kinds of programs we watch, and the books we choose to read. We need to take a rest from social media and the news and reflect on how information impacts us and our well-being. In order to put everything into perspective, we have to mix up our information intake with positive news, such as inspiring stories and new inventions that can motivate us.

WHAT TYPE OF MINDSET YOU HAVE

Our chances of success are significantly influenced by our own mindset. We have the ability to transform the restrictive thinking that is stopping us from improving. Dr. Carol Dweck, a psychologist at Stanford University, introduced the idea of fixed and growth mindsets through her studies on how humans handle problems and challenges (Abdou, 2022).

- Fixed mindset: If someone has a fixed mindset, they think that some traits, such as talent and intelligence, are innate and permanent. They typically believe that they will never be good at anything if they are not good at it now.
- Growth mindset: If someone has a growth mindset, they will believe that intelligence and talent can always be improved through practice and hard work.

It should come as no surprise that our mindset greatly affects our ambition, persistence, and success. It is also obvious that adopting a growth mindset can help us become disciplined in our work because we will always try to improve ourselves. We have no control over our circumstances, but we do have power over our mentality. We should strive to cultivate a growth-oriented mindset since we can achieve our goals and face problems by working hard and keeping an open mind.

REALIZING WHEN TO LOOK FOR HELP

Humans are social beings, and supporting one another helps us succeed. We should never isolate ourselves or drive people away if we are experiencing overwhelming and uncontrollable feelings. Rather, admit that we need support and help from others. Then, we should take action to obtain it. We will overcome obstacles and achieve our goals more quickly if we have a support system. For example, if we have a major project at work that we will not be able to finish by ourselves, we have to get assistance from our coworkers so that we can avoid burnout. We can also get inspiration from a mentor or professional coach if we ever need help making a hard decision. In order to keep a positive attitude and make wise judgments as we go through life, it can be helpful to seek out inspirational people to guide us.

KEY TAKEAWAYS

- Attempting to control everything in life is a losing battle. Don't waste your energy on things you cannot change any more. You will get stuck and become stagnant if you try to force control over things that are out of your reach.
- However, there are some parts of life that we can take control of, such as how we communicate with our loved ones, how we maintain our mental health, how we respond when something negative happens, what we do with our free time, what kind of news we watch, what type of mindset we have, and when to look for help.
- If we gain control of what is in our power, we will be able to significantly improve the quality of our lives.
- Furthermore, in order to take charge of the aspects we are able to control, we can pay close attention to our feelings and emotions, concentrate on the present by trying to practice mindfulness, and take action to create change.

6

TAKING RESPONSIBILITY FOR EVERYTHING THAT HAPPENS IN YOUR LIFE, WHETHER GOOD OR BAD

"The moment you take responsibility for everything in your life, is the moment you can change anything in your life."- Hal Elrod

WHY DO YOU NEED TO TAKE RESPONSIBILITY FOR YOUR LIFE?

Our lives are entirely our responsibility. We must acknowledge this if we plan to have consistent self-discipline and accomplish success in our lives and careers. A lot of people believe that everything and everyone else is to blame. For example, in the workplace, where people are connected so intricately and each project has a chain of internal clients who are dependent on one another, it is very easy to come up with excuses for why a problem is not their responsibility. Failure is never the outcome of the decisions they took; each failure has a scapegoat that they may use to avoid taking accountability for their own conduct (Heathfield, 2020).

What happens when we refuse to take responsibility? We are more inclined to view our lives as a failure if we do not take ownership of our own actions because we let the wind blow us around and then blame it for how things played out. We create an unhappy life—one that does not satisfy any of our hopes and expectations—when we fail to appropriately guide our paths and achievements.

Moreover, when we avoid responsibility for the things that happen in our lives, we risk causing other issues, such as pessimistic thoughts, a victimized mindset, constant disagreements, hesitation, stagnancy, and codependency. When we take responsibility, more favorable outcomes are bound to come our way. We have to be careful about the choices and decisions we make if we aspire to a higher quality of life that makes us happy and successful.

Are you driven by a fierce passion? Or do you have a mediocre lens through which you see your reality? Whatever improvements we desire, we have to first assume responsibility for our lives and never completely entrust anyone else with them. When we put our lives in the hands of others, we give others the authority and permission to guide our lives in whatever way they see fit, often at the cost of our own improvement. We do not wish this to happen to us, which is why it is important to start taking responsibility for our own lives.

While taking full responsibility entails holding ourselves completely accountable, it does not imply being alone and living a secluded life separated from other people. It's okay if we accept assistance from others even as we accept full responsibility for our own lives. We can ask for their opinions or that they hold us accountable. Strong social ties play a significant role in helping to create long-lasting happiness for a lot of people. Rather than assuming that other people will understand our needs or wait for them to change, we must also take responsibility for our relationships.

HOW DO YOU TAKE RESPONSIBILITY?
PRIORITIZING YOURSELF

We must first believe that we are deserving of a great life in order to make smarter decisions and take responsibility for our lives. Due to self-limiting beliefs, many people fear taking responsibility. As a result, these people can think that they do not deserve better. We need to keep in mind that occasionally being selfish is not wrong. If we are not giving ourselves love and support, how can we expect others to do the same?

We can prioritize ourselves by engaging in self-love and self-care practices. Loving ourselves can boost our confidence and helps us realize that we have the final say in how we desire our lives to go. A ten-minute meditation, journaling, a warm bath, gardening, and repeating uplifting mantras each day are instances of self-love and self-care practices. To give another example, on the weekends, we can take ourselves to go shopping or go to a spa to reward ourselves for our hard work during the weekdays.

NOT PLACING BLAME ON OTHERS

Stopping the blame game is the first step in taking responsibility for our lives. Why? Because if you do not accept responsibility for your life, you are probably blaming other people or circumstances for your problems. It is always anything other than yourself that is to blame, whether it is a dysfunctional relationship, a difficult childhood, financial difficulties, or other challenges that inevitably happen with life. It is true that life can be unfair. Some people are more unlucky than others. In some situations, you may also be the victim. Even so, what exactly does blaming others accomplish? Playing the victim card? Justification for the unpleasant circumstances of life?

Blaming actually only leads to anger, frustration, and helplessness. The people you point the finger at are usually unaware of your feelings or do not even care. The truth is that while such emotions and feelings may be valid, they will never advance our success or happiness. Getting rid of the blame does not excuse others' unfair conduct. It also does not disregard the challenges of life. However, what we have to know is that our lives are about us and not them. In order to regain the freedom and power that are rightfully ours, we must stop the blame game.

BEING WARY OF EXCUSES

People that are irresponsible frequently find or create a variety of excuses for their actions. An irresponsible individual who desires to make healthier choices might claim that they are unable to do so because they do not have the time. The thing is they could find the time to do it if only they were responsible. There are countless reasons for not making life changes. However, when we let them stop us from changing anything, that reason turns into an excuse.

Trying to make excuses prevents us from having the chance to grow from our mistakes. There is no room for growth when there is no personal responsibility. Without ever moving ahead, we will be trapped in the same place whining and obsessing over the negative things. We will be able to put an end to negativity when we take responsibility for our lives and refrain from making excuses. We will come to the realization that external circumstances are meaningless and our actions are the only thing that truly matters.

REMOVING TOXIC PEOPLE

Genuinely loving and caring people will hold us accountable because they wish to see us succeed in life. Toxic people may wish to prevent us from achieving our goals in order to keep us dependent on them. In this scenario, these people are not our true friends, so we need to remove them from our lives.

We must be responsible for the people we choose to surround ourselves with if we want to take responsibility for our lives. People who frequently criticize, self-loathe, speak poorly of themselves, and complain about our success are not good for our improvement. These people will hinder our progress. We should only maintain interactions that are constructive and healthy. Furthermore, we should work to achieve emotional independence so that we can make better decisions objectively and draw genuine people into our lives.

FOCUSING ON TAKING ACTION

Everybody has their own goals and dreams, but without taking any action, they will never be realized. What good is it to talk about doing something but never follow through? It is impossible to accept responsibility without any action that follows. Our lives will get better even if we just take baby steps in the right direction. We should never forget that our habits are where the action begins. As time passes by, taking small steps every day adds up to a huge step in the end.

LOVING YOURSELF

If we have trouble taking responsibility for ourselves and our actions, it is probably because we do not value ourselves either. Why is this? Because those with very low self-esteem typically do not take responsibility. Rather, the responsibility and blame are placed on others, which fosters a victim mentality. We will not be able to improve our self-esteem until we recognize that we have made mistakes and take responsibility for them. Being responsible gives us the ability to take initiative to better ourselves and other people around us.

If we depend on outside reinforcement in order to boost our self-esteem, such as getting compliments from other people, it means that we give away the power to them. Instead, we should work on developing internal stability. We must know how to value ourselves and who we are as people. When we can love ourselves, there is no other choice but to take responsibility for our lives. Since it is our own reality, the best way to enhance it is for us to take responsibility for our behavior.

GETTING RID OF NEGATIVE SELF-TALK

In order to start taking responsibility, we need to eliminate negative self-talk. Negative self-talk may originate from childhood trauma brought on by abuse in the home or being bullied at school (Murphy, 2021). For instance, if you are body shamed and insulted by bullies as a child, eventually you will start to believe them, which makes you feel horrible and insecure about yourself. These negative, self-restricting beliefs we have about ourselves are frequently the result of projections and judgments made by others (Murphy, 2021). These statements have a tendency to be internalized while we are younger, and as a result, they stick with us as we grow older. It will take some time to break such ingrained negative self-perceptions. However, it is achievable through engaging in self-love and self-care practices.

ACKNOWLEDGING NEGATIVE EMOTIONS

A lot of people find it difficult to accept this. Everyone wants to feel happy and have positive emotions, after all. However, we also need to be responsible for our emotions if we are going to start taking responsibility for ourselves. The fact is that nobody can always be positive and upbeat. Everybody has a dark side in them. The darker side of life will hit us harder in the future if we always ignore or repress it. It is important to be honest about who we are deep inside because we will never improve or be successful in life if we always try to be someone that we are not. In order to be self-disciplined, we need to take responsibility for ourselves no matter the cost.

CULTIVATING COMPASSION FOR YOURSELF

Since we know that we are able to choose the course that our lives can take, taking full responsibility can be challenging. After knowing this fact, some of us may become a little harsh on ourselves. Unfortunately, a lot of us are our own worst critics. We disturb our inner balance when we are being critical of ourselves, and the discouragement that we experience as a result can also make us feel depressed and hopeless about our situations. In order to resolve the issue, we need to cultivate self-compassion. We should try to say positive things to (or about) ourselves and see the humor in the circumstances. By the same token, we should feel thankful for having learned the lesson rather than feeling guilty or resentful. We can discover the wisdom in what we have learned about ourselves instead of feeling like we have wasted our time. When we take responsibility for our lives, even a simple change in perspective can have a significant impact.

NOT INTERNALIZING JUDGMENT

Everybody always has their own opinion about things. However, we should not internalize the judgments that other people have about us. Each of us has our own stance on happiness and success that makes us unique. Even though a lot of our loved ones have the best intentions, they often try to project their own wishes onto us. For instance, some parents may insist that their children choose a particular major in college, career path, or even partner in marriage. We cannot live our lives in order to please others. We are all responsible for living our own lives.

Rather than internalizing the opinions and judgments of others, we should put more effort into getting to know who we are. What do success and happiness seem like in our eyes? What criteria do we use to find a love partner? We have better, more fulfilling lives when we are honest about who we are as people. We must therefore be absolutely honest with ourselves if we want to succeed. It may even be necessary for us to spend some time away from those who are continuously forcing their opinions on us because this can lead to internal conflict and make decision-making extremely difficult.

TAKING RESPONSIBILITY EVEN IF IT IS NOT YOUR FAULT

The more you decide to take responsibility for your life, the more control you will have over it. The first thing to do in order to resolve our problems in life is to take responsibility for them. Due to the misconception that accepting responsibility for our problems also involves accepting fault, many people are reluctant to do so. In our culture, responsibility, and fault frequently go hand in hand. However, they are distinct from one another. For example, if you hit someone with your car, you are both at fault and most certainly have a legal obligation to compensate them. Although hitting that person was not intentional, you would still be the one responsible for it. In this society, fault works out that way. We are responsible for making things right whenever we make a mistake, and that is also how it ought to be.

However, there are also other issues that are not our fault but for which we still bear responsibility. For instance, if you have a business and you are the boss of your company, you will have employees working for you. When someone makes a mistake, let's say an error that causes your company to lose over 1 million dollars, you are the one who has hired that employee. In this case, you will be 100% responsible for that 1-million-dollar mistake, and not that employee. If you had been more careful about who you decided to hire, the company would probably have never lost that money. You accept the consequences that would happen when you chose to hire someone.

As another example, perhaps one day the town you live in is left without electricity, and you are not able to do the things you usually do. Who do you think is responsible for that? Of course, you are. You decided to live in that town and also chose not to buy a generator for your house. Once you accept this fact, you can either move to a different city or get yourself a generator.

All the time, we bear responsibility for things that are not our fault, and this is a fact that we must accept. Fault is in the past and responsibility is in the present. Fault comes from decisions that have previously been made. However, responsibility comes from decisions that we are making every single day.

There is a distinction between holding somebody else responsible for our circumstances and simply blaming them. We alone are responsible for our situations in life. Our misery may be caused by different people, but we are ultimately the ones responsible for our own happiness. This is because we can always decide how we see things and how we respond to them.

KEY TAKEAWAYS

- Self-disciplined people take responsibility for their lives, and instead of blaming others refrain from pointing fingers before understanding your situation.
- Whatever changes we seek, we must first take charge of our lives and never fully leave them to someone else. Accepting responsibility ultimately entails changing the direction of our lives in order to experience greater fulfillment and more beneficial outcomes.
- As explained above, there are some steps we can take to assume responsibilities, such as prioritizing ourselves, being wary of excuses, removing toxic people, focusing on taking action, loving ourselves, getting rid of negative self-talk, acknowledging the existence of negative emotions, and not internalizing judgment.
- In American culture, responsibility and fault often go hand in hand. However, they are two different things. The fault is in the past; responsibility is in the present. This is why when you take responsibility for something it does not mean that it is necessarily your fault. Taking responsibility means that we agree to be responsible to fix the problems so we can become better.

7

PRACTICING DELAYED GRATIFICATION

"The ability to discipline yourself to delay gratification in the short term in order to enjoy greater rewards in the long term, is the indispensable prerequisite for success."- Brian Tracy

WHAT IS DELAYED GRATIFICATION?

Having something that we desire right away feels great. However, there are times when doing something to feel good or to prevent discomfort costs us what we really want out of life. These longer-term objectives serve as a reward for delayed gratification. The goals do not even have to be that far into the future, yet they can bring us greater happiness or shield us from more suffering than the gratification we get from the present moment.

What exactly is delayed gratification? It is the capacity to resist the temptation of immediate pleasure in hopes of a greater or even more lasting reward in the future (Waters, 2021). When we know how to delay gratification, we can hold off until we finally get what we really want. Its opposite is instant satisfaction; instead of being patient and waiting for what we really desire, we choose something that will make us happy immediately.

Instant gratification is accepted as the norm in the age of one-click transactions and instantly available information. The idea that we must have what we want immediately is reinforced by the tech world where we have our internet and smartphones at all times. Instant gratification, however, is not always the greatest option; in fact, delayed gratification is a crucial life skill that we must learn. When it comes to having consistent self-discipline to reach our goals, delayed gratification is an ability that will get us there more quickly.

The truth is that expecting to achieve everything we desire, much less instantly, is impossible. Since it raises unrealistic expectations, instant gratification is essentially a starting point of frustration. Developing the ability to delay gratification allows us to gain time to plan things carefully and also learn from our failures.

The Marshmallow Test

THE MARSHMALLOW TEST

Walter Mischel, a professor at Stanford, came up with one of the better examples of delayed gratification in the 1960s (Robbins, 2022). He experimented on young children by putting every one of them in a room with just a marshmallow on a table. He then made a deal with every kid that if they held off on eating the marshmallow while he momentarily left the room, he would give them another marshmallow. However, there would not be another marshmallow if the child decided to eat the first one.

The findings of the infamous Marshmallow Test showed how challenging it is for humans of all ages to delay gratification. Some kids gobbled up the first marshmallow right away. Others made an effort to exercise self-control but ended up giving up. Only a handful of kids were able to resist and receive the second marshmallow prize.

The researchers then followed the Marshmallow Test participants into adulthood for over 40 years (Navidad, 2020). The kids who chose to delay their reward were much more successful in practically all aspects of their lives than those who gave in to the first marshmallow. Moreover, they also possessed greater social skills, became healthier, performed better on their tests, reacted much better to anxiety and stress, as well as had fewer drug problems (Robbins, 2022). This illustration of delayed gratification showed how important it is to reach our goals and accomplish more in essentially every area of life.

HERE ARE A FEW OF THE BENEFITS OF PRACTICING DELAYED GRATIFICATION

ACHIEVING LONG-TERM SUCCESS

When pursuing long-term objectives in both our personal and professional lives, we often have to make certain decisions. Do we spend our time watching a YouTube video or completing our homework? Should we waste our money on new clothes or save it for a nicer apartment? Do we choose to browse through Instagram or finish our project at work? Choosing what seems harder suggests at least some form of delayed gratification. More benefits result from doing so regularly than we would get in the short term. We will be able to achieve success over longer periods when we are willing to give up the pleasure we are currently enjoying in order to work toward our future goals. Delaying gratification allows us to hit more of our long-term targets and thus demonstrate to ourselves that we are capable of completing these tasks. We may feel better about ourselves as a result. For example, when you have a project assigned to you, you will want to create high-quality work within the time frame given to make your superior satisfied. In order to achieve that goal, you will need to avoid postponing doing the project and pour your heart into it. Once you are able to present great work and get complimented because of it, you will feel good about yourself and trust your ability more than before, which leads to greater self-worth.

HAVING IMPROVED HEALTH

In the Marshmallow Test, it was discovered that children who were more open to waiting for long periods for their reward would go on to have better long-term health. This is perhaps because they have the ability to delay gratification rather than fall into the temptation of bad behaviors. For instance, they may be more skilled at controlling their urges to smoke, consume unhealthy foods, put off exercising, and drink excessively.

GREATER MENTAL STABILITY

As you consolidate your ability to chase long-term rewards instead of short-term distractions, you'll also improve your mental health and well-being. Once you demonstrate a greater mental stability, staying the course to achieve distant goals becomes much easier.

Nevertheless, you will gain a new level of emotional intelligence.

EXAMPLES OF DELAYED GRATIFICATION

What does delayed gratification appear like? Depending on the area of life, it can take many different forms. Let's examine several instances of delayed gratification so that we can practice it more.

PERSONAL LIFE

Regardless of our weight, improving our nutrition is a long-term commitment that can help us become healthier as we age. However, it calls for a great deal of delayed gratification. It may feel nice at the moment to overeat or indulge in tempting foods that do not properly nourish our bodies. The greater reward, though, is healthy nourishment, which is difficult to attain for a lot of people. Put differently, we get to experience the gratification of being healthier as opposed to constantly consuming tasty but unhealthy meals and feeling satisfied for a moment only. We, therefore, have to be able to resist the need to indulge in unhealthy foods right away and focus on our long-term goals of maintaining good health.

PROFESSIONAL LIFE

Let's say that we are working to get a promotion at work. We are all aware that in order to accomplish this, we will have to hone the skills that define a strong leader. Even when we do not always feel like doing it, we must develop these skills outside of work if we want to see some improvement. It is very easy to fall prey to instant gratification and waste our evenings binge-watching our favorite TV programs. However, doing that will not pay off in the long term. Rather, we will need to invest some time in improving ourselves in order to receive the greater advantage of a promotion. This can help us develop as a leader and increase our likelihood of attaining our long-term professional ambitions.

INTERPERSONAL LIFE

There is an equal amount of giving and receiving in any healthy relationship. Our needs cannot always come first when we are trying to develop a relationship with somebody else. We may occasionally have to give in so as to build a long-lasting partnership that is advantageous to both sides. If someone they care about needs them, those with an instant gratification mentality may prioritize their own needs over their partner's. Delaying gratification, on the contrary, enables both sides to cooperate in order to create a positive, equal partnership.

THE STEPS TO BECOMING BETTER AT DELAYING GRATIFICATION

Delaying gratification is difficult at a time when distractions are all around us. It can be challenging to resist the temptation of Facebook, Instagram, TikTok, and Netflix. When companies are competing for our valuable attention, how can we maintain our discipline? In order to answer this question, here are some steps that can be utilized in order to be better at delaying gratification.

KNOWING WHAT YOU WANT

Everybody aspires to success, but not everyone actually accomplishes it. We need to first determine our intentions and desires in order to increase our chances. Finding a goal from our current passions is a fantastic place to start, and here are a few examples:

- Having money and material possessions.
- Obtaining a happy state of mind.
- Preserving physical health.
- Positively impacting others.
- Exploring or learning something new.
- Being efficient with time and productive.
- Establishing connections and making acquaintances.

What do you think your life's work is? Commit to your goals by putting them in writing. The actual work starts once we have made up our minds about what we want to achieve in life.

BEGINNING WITH A SMALL THING

It is not necessary to begin exercising our ability to delay gratification because of something that will happen years from now. We should start off small and work toward our larger, longer-term objectives after that. The gratification for a small thing should still be delayed, even though we only have to wait a short period of time before receiving it. How long we should wait relies on our capacity for delayed gratification. For example, if we struggle to wait a week for a reward, we may start with one day only. As time passes by, we will be able to incorporate the habit into our lives gradually. If we do not have anything specific we want to work toward, we can establish it in our lives.

Here is one instance. Say you want to get better at public speaking at your office. Your practice will not immediately provide good results. However, you may give yourself a break by doing something enjoyable as a reward for practicing public speaking every day. This can involve watching an episode of your favorite Netflix show. As a consequence, if you do not practice, it means that you cannot watch any episode that day; then you will have to wait another day to get that reward. You can then increase your tolerance as time goes on. Perhaps following a couple of weeks of honing your public speaking skill, you can reward yourself with a trip to the spa or the salon.

TAKING A BREAK FROM SOCIAL MEDIA

This may appear to have nothing to do with delayed gratification, but it is actually not true. When was the last time you went through Instagram or Facebook without ending up at an external website to look at an online shop? Social media influencers have a reason for doing what they do on the internet, and these apps were purposefully created with that in mind. Since social media is a relatable thing for people of all ages, it is the most effective kind of marketing. The more we browse through it, the more we will feel as though we need a product to be as happy as the people we see on the internet. For instance, a lot of us are probably guilty of buying unnecessary skincare and beauty products in an effort to resemble our favorite social media influencers.

However, if we desire to learn to delay gratification, removing a key stimulus for routinely gratifying ourselves instantly is a terrific way to do this. For instance, we can perhaps take a week or two off social media. As another example, if Instagram is a major trigger for us, we can take it further by deactivating or deleting our account. We need to be aware of how it impacts our impulses. Once we are aware of these triggers and impulses, we can avoid them much better and learn to put off our urges for delayed gratification.

THINKING ABOUT THE REAL COST

Asking ourselves this question will allow us to delay gratification more successfully: What does the thing or the action we are going to perform actually cost? For instance, if we are about to make a significant purchase from an online shop, we can make an effort to estimate how many hours of work it will need. We will start to second-guess ourselves when we realize that one item might equal a week of work to do. As another illustration, if we are about to consume a whole bucket of ice cream in one sitting, we have to think of all the possible costs to our health. This can result in a significant blood sugar increase that will undoubtedly result in various stomach problems. The real cost of instant reward may not always be worth it at all. We all need to think about the cost and decide if the momentary pleasure is actually worth it to us.

KEY TAKEAWAYS

- Delayed gratification refers to the ability to resist the temptation of immediate pleasure. We avoid temptation because we anticipate a bigger or longer-lasting reward down the road.
- As demonstrated by the Marshmallow Test, the children who decided to wait for more rewards became more successful in their lives as they grew up. This is because they knew how to control their impulses and did not give in to instant gratification easily. From this experiment, we learn how important it is to practice delayed gratification more in our lives.
- There are some benefits that can be gained from practicing delayed gratification, such as achieving stronger self-worth, having improved health, and getting long-term success.
- Tips on becoming better at delaying gratification: knowing what you want, beginning with a small thing, taking a break from social media, and thinking about the real cost. If we follow these tips, we will be able to wait for better future rewards, which can lead to having consistent self-discipline as well.

8

IGNORING THE NAYSAYERS

"Ignore the naysayers. They don't know what they're talking about when it comes to your life." - Maria Lesetz

WHAT ARE NAYSAYERS?

Naysayers are people who like to express their negative or pessimistic views and project them onto others (Khurana, 2021). No matter where we are on the grand game board of life, we will encounter individuals who, to put it bluntly, have less-than-good motives at some point. We will always have those people rooting for us, like our family and friends, who support whatever we do. They want to be present to share our achievements with us because they want those things for us and are confident they will happen in the first place. But there are also some who are being negative about everything. They constantly seem to be in our lives and enjoy pointing out our shortcomings and how we will fail in what we dream to accomplish.

When we tell the naysayers what we wish for in life, they often start doubting us and our ability to succeed, thus discouraging us from even attempting to try something. They typically lack the knowledge necessary to determine our chances of success, but they will try to talk us out of our plans and convince us that we will fail. It truly does not matter what these negative people think and what their opinions are, regardless of their motivations. Oftentimes, they will advise against trying something since they tried it and ended in failure. But someone is not automatically an expert just because they tried it once, failed to achieve it, and decided to give up.

Even while there is a general sense that things are going well, a few naysayers will try to cast pessimism, which can result in hindering our progress. Every time we are getting sidetracked by naysayers, it is simply because we have lost focus on the goals that we have set. If so, all we have to do is take a look at them again. We need to remind ourselves what we desire to do specifically. We must also think about what it is that we truly wish for our lives. If we are dealing with naysayers, we have to first realize that we are in control of our own lives and do not need negative people telling us what we must do.

Arnold Schwarzenegger has taken to heart Nelson Mandela's belief that "It always seems to be impossible until someone does it." Schwarzenegger wanted to break new records and do something that no one else had ever done, and he actually accomplished what he set out to do. What he did seemed impossible, and he probably had to ignore a couple of naysayers, but he kept going until he achieved what he wanted.

THE REASONS TO IGNORE THE NAYSAYERS
STOPPING NEGATIVITY FROM CREEPING INTO YOUR MIND

The strength of positive thinking is real. Although it might sound like a thing from fictional stories, a lot can actually be achieved simply by maintaining a positive mindset. This way of thinking keeps us going when things get tough and also makes us stay away from the naysayers in the process. By being optimistic, we will be able to persuade people to support us or change their minds, which will let us take control of the matter. For the precise reason that it fosters more success, some people even describe a positive attitude as a development mindset (Olenski, 2018).

For example, great leaders have a method of preventing negativity from affecting them. In the business world, all sorts of unpleasant events might occur, but leaders cannot allow these things to get them down. If a leader always appears depressed, angry, displeased, or sad, their team will not be able to count on them to be the presence that the team members need. To great leaders, naysayers cannot be fully ignored because occasionally they may provide insightful feedback. However, rather than dwelling on that negativity, great leaders will first recognize the perspective before turning to a more positive path. Negativity can consume our entire being if we let it because it serves only as a roadblock on the way to our success.

PREVENTING YOU FROM ABANDONING YOUR DREAM

Nobody wants to wonder about what could have occurred if they had pursued their goal rather than just letting somebody convince them not to do it. This kind of regret will lead us to hatred and resentment. If we realize that somebody else uses that idea that we have thought about, proceeded with it, and is now incredibly successful, we can feel upset and resentful.

We all know about Jeff Bezos, the founder of Amazon and one of the richest men on earth. He once said that he knew that if he had failed, he would not have regretted that, but a thing he would definitely regret was not trying at all. Even though we may dislike and even hate the person who persuaded us that our goals will never come true, we will resent ourselves even more for following their opinion and allowing them to determine our lives' fate. If Jeff Bezos and his vision of the greatest online shop in the world have turned out to be successful, there is no excuse we cannot accomplish our own ambitions by not listening to the naysayers.

MOTIVATING OTHER PEOPLE TO IGNORE THEIR NAYSAYERS

We can serve as a motivation and role model for others with our relentless determination to achieve success in the face of difficulties. For example, internet influencers these days have become a crucial part of modern marketing because what reputable people do and say is shaping more and more how individuals make decisions in their lives. While influencers frequently affect people's shopping choices, they can also be a factor in different kinds of decisions, such as whether or not someone should transform an idea into a real business.

For instance, if we aspire to instill motivation in business for others, a great way to start is to volunteer as a mentor to young entrepreneurs. We can try to share our success stories in various schools and online learning classes. We may also join a mentorship group to help others who are dealing with the same naysayers get beyond the obstacles just as we did. Moreover, if we want to become social media influencers, we can open up an Instagram or YouTube account and post videos about our success journeys there. We will be able to influence other people positively by paving our own path to success first.

WAYS TO IGNORE THE NAYSAYERS

DEFINING YOUR DREAM CLEARLY

We will be more likely to stick to our goals in the face of challenges if we describe them clearly. We need to be more specific here. What precisely does the dream look like? How will we know when we have succeeded in reaching our goals? We have to clearly envisage this. For example, if you are good at programming and wish to create a new game, you will have to know what kind of game you want to make. You need to think about how the game will play out and where the market you want to promote it is. Perhaps you will think that you have reached the goal when the game is finished being programmed or when it brings you some profits. When you can define your goal, it will be much easier for you to start.

KNOWING WHY YOU ARE DOING IT

Why is this dream important? There is no correct response to this question. Simply being able to respond to it and having an answer that inspires us to take action is what matters. Our motivation to keep going will increase when our reasons for wanting to realize our ambitions become stronger. Let's take the example above.

You wish to create a new game, but why do you want to do this? What is your endgame? Do you wish to get as much profit as possible and make your own game company? Do you only do it for fun because it is your passion? Whatever your reasons, you need to know them first.

FIGHTING YOUR INNER NAYSAYERS

We might be the worst critic of ourselves. Our inner naysayers are the voice inside of us telling us we will not be able to accomplish our future goals because we are not clever enough, wealthy enough, lucky enough, or connected with the right people, among other things. We must silence all these negative voices and replace them with one that is empowering in reminding us that we can do everything because we are smart, hard-working, and strong enough to accomplish it.

SURROUNDING YOURSELF WITH POSITIVE INDIVIDUALS

In large part, we will become just like the people we are with. We will probably become negative people if we only hang out with negative individuals in our lives. We will benefit from surrounding ourselves with people who are pursuing their goals, facing their fears, and improving their skills. The people we choose to have around us play a big role in determining who we are or want to be. When you were young, your parents may have warned you not to hang out with the kids who drank alcohol or did drugs because they might have a bad influence on you. Your parents were definitely in the right here since these kids would try to convince others to do what they did or you would think that you were not cool enough if you did not engage in these activities.

NOT THINKING ABOUT YOUR PLANS TOO MUCH

Planning too much is not good because actions are actually much more crucial than plans. We should not get too caught up in having the ideal plan before we start because 99.9% of every plan ends up changing as we are doing it. We need to make a move as soon as we can. We should start when the idea pops up in our heads and make changes later on. As long as we are clear in defining our goals, we will be able to accomplish them successfully. For instance, you want to make a clothing business and have made all the designs. You may also know what materials you would like to use on the clothes. In this scenario, you should just start finding tailors to make samples for your clothes instead of thinking about it too much. On the way, if you do not like how the designs are or you think that the materials are not good enough, you can just change them as you see fit before finally ordering the final products.

BEING READY TO FAIL

Failure is not a thing because it does not exist; instead, there are just outcomes. It is as simple as that to take new action if the previous ones do not produce the desired results. We need to get over our failure-related fears. We should get out there and fail quickly and frequently so that we can learn from our mistakes and advance as time passes. We should never stop trying because we do not get what we want on the first try. What we should do is try again, no matter how many times we make mistakes. Let's take a look at Suzy Batiz, for example. Batiz experienced two periods of bankruptcy prior to founding the $240 million brand Poo-Pourri toilet spray (Castrillon, 2019). She sought to start a business from scratch, as she was enthusiastic about the industry. However, that did not work out at first because, at the age of 21, she made her first bankruptcy filing. Batiz refused to give in to the difficult circumstances. She established the Poo-Pourri toilet spray business after filing for bankruptcy for the second time, and it became a big success. She ultimately managed to rank among America's Richest Self-Made Women in 2019 as a result of her company's good advertising strategy (Castrillon, 2019).

KEY TAKEAWAYS

- If we wish to accomplish our goals and have consistent self-discipline, we will have to ignore all the naysayers that are around us. All they do is bring negativity into our lives and hinder our future success.
- Naysayers want us to believe that our ideas and ambitions are just in our heads and are not possible to put into action. This is why we need to remove them from our lives so that we will become more positive and will not have any regrets later on.
- Tips for ignoring the naysayers: defining your dream clearly, knowing why you are pursuing it, fighting your inner naysayers, surrounding yourself with positive individuals, not thinking about your plans too much, and being ready to fail.

9

FINDING A MENTOR TO EMULATE

"A mentor empowers a person to see a possible future, and believe it can be obtained."- Shawn Hitchcock

In a mentoring relationship, an experienced person (the mentor) shares their knowledge, skills, and wisdom with a less experienced person (the mentee) all while developing their own mentoring abilities (D'Angelo, 2022). In mentorship, proper guidance is provided to the mentee while still keeping a friendly and encouraging relationship with the mentor.

Someone can be considered a mentor when they have succeeded in the goal that we wish to achieve. It means that they have mastered the ways to have consistent self-discipline in order to accomplish that goal. Therefore, if we set a goal, it is essential that we find ourselves a mentor who can give us advice and tips on how to accomplish it. When we have little experience, we may occasionally feel confused when pursuing our goals. A mentor, however, has years or decades of practical experience in our field and can help us develop our abilities and learn valuable lessons from (Roepe, 2022). Finding a mentor then is one of the most powerful moves we can do to change our lives.

THE BENEFITS OF HAVING A MENTOR

There are several advantages to mentoring for us. We can discover new things, expand our networks, and improve our self-discipline by establishing this relationship. We can determine whether or not we wish to find a mentor by considering these benefits.

HAVING SOMEONE TO SUPPORT YOUR GROWTH

Mentors support and empower the growth of another person's improvement. A mentor can help us to concentrate our efforts by providing feedback and setting goals. For this reason, many companies often develop mentorship programs in order to hone the skills of their employees. Employees like working environments that support professional growth because it shows that their employer cares about them and intends to see them succeed.

TAPPING INTO A SOURCE OF KNOWLEDGE

Mentors can offer us specialized knowledge and perspectives that help us succeed. They provide guidance on how to carry out specific tasks or acquire practical skills, for instance. Such advice can be helpful to those who are just starting their professional careers because it enables them to become more at ease in their positions more quickly and perhaps get promoted more easily. For example, you are about to start a new company. When you have a mentor on your side, they will be able to teach you how to create your preliminary business and financial plan. It means that you will not have to spend so much time researching about it because your mentor can provide it for you easily.

MAINTAINING ACCOUNTABILITY

Mentors support their mentees by holding them accountable for their goals. A mentor can keep us motivated and on course to fulfill our goals by monitoring our progress as we go along. In addition, they can make sure that we do not lose sight of our ambitions. Having someone who keeps an eye on us can help to motivate and hold us accountable since we do not want to disappoint our mentors by failing to accomplish our goals. For example, if you start to procrastinate or get discouraged in your efforts, a mentor will remind you why you need to keep going because you need to be responsible for yourself and your life.

PROVIDING ENCOURAGEMENT

We can seek assistance from our mentors when we are having trouble completing a task or achieving a goal. We may be inspired to keep going forward in the face of obstacles by this support and encouragement. In order to instill confidence in us, our mentors might also recognize and remind us of our strengths and skills.

When we can radiate confidence, we will be less inclined to give up on our ambitions and dreams.

HELPING CREATE NEW CONNECTIONS

A mentor can support us in expanding our network and connection. They can introduce us to potential opportunities or people who will be able to help us when we can identify our career or personal goals. For example, if we want career advancement at work, these kinds of connections are helpful for us because our mentors often have more experience in the business or more senior positions as well. A mentor can lead us to the right people in pursuit of our goals so that we do not have to start from the beginning by ourselves.

HAVING SOMEONE WILLING TO LISTEN TO YOU

When we get an idea in our heads, we can share it with a mentor to discuss or debate it. Thanks to their relevant knowledge and experience, a mentor can provide us with honest guidance and suggestions about what we need to do. These insights help us decide whether or not to go along with that idea or abandon it, as well as what strategies to take. Furthermore, a mentor can also assist us with day-to-day issues. For example, if you have a project-related conflict with your boss at work, you can turn to your mentor for guidance on what measures to take because they will listen to you before offering advice.

GETTING CONSTRUCTIVE FEEDBACK

Genuine feedback can be given in a mentoring relationship built on trust. By developing trust, we will be able to learn that constructive feedback from our mentors is meant to advance our development instead of hurting our personal feelings. Our mentors can help us by pointing out areas for improvement and any shortcomings we might need to overcome. Since this is a professional connection, our mentors have objective roles to fulfill. Our friends or colleagues can be reluctant to point up our flaws because they do not want to come off as judgmental. For example, if you have an impossible idea that you think will work out, your friends may not be willing to talk too much about it lest you take their words the wrong way and think that they are being negative to you. However, a mentor will be able to give you honest comments on the idea since you trust them and their intentions.

PROVIDING GUIDELINES

If we have just started our careers, a mentor can help us establish guidelines for what is expected of us professionally. For instance, they might make clear the importance of the position and acceptable workplace conduct. These guidelines may assist us in forming productive work habits that will help us concentrate and complete our tasks successfully. We will be able to increase our productivity and impress our bosses with these productive work practices.

HAVING A TRUSTED ALLY

A crucial aspect of mentoring partnerships is trust. We have to have faith in our mentors and trust that they will offer accurate and sincere advice as well as have our best interests in mind. We both must be able to rely on each other to keep secret information private. In order to build trust in the relationship, our mentors have to be able to keep their word and communicate frequently. For instance, if you are planning to implement a new business idea and run it by your mentor, they will have to keep all information about it confidential so that no one can steal that idea from you. Given how fierce the competition is in the business sector, a mentor whom we can trust is very important to have.

HOW TO FIND AND ESTABLISH A RELATIONSHIP WITH A MENTOR

KNOWING WHAT A MENTOR IS AND IS NOT

As explained above, a mentor is an individual who can support and empower us, urge us to seek out new prospects, and assist us in overcoming obstacles, such as changing roles or accepting a difficult job. For example, a mentor may be someone who works in the same field as us or a person in the profession type of role we wish to change into. This person can serve as our mentor and provide advice on how to enhance our careers or work. Although it is possible to receive mentorship from a friend, generally mentors will be at least one or two career levels higher than us (Patel, 2022). We need to remember that a mentor is not the same as a sponsor. A sponsor utilizes their connections to actively support a younger or less experienced individual's professional progress, while a mentor provides guidance and addresses concerns (Roepe, 2022).

We generally think of mentorship as a long-term, one-on-one connection between a mentor and mentee, but that is actually not the only possibility. Peer mentoring with somebody on the same level as us and group mentoring where we do not meet one-on-one are only two examples of the various types of mentoring available out there (Krbechek & Tagle, 2022). Additionally, mentoring can be done on small levels. For example, you look up to a colleague at work who has a good performance. In order to learn more about their experiences or to get advice on how to perform better at work, you can ask them to have a one-time mentoring session with you.

BEING SPECIFIC ABOUT YOUR GOAL

We should think about what we intend to gain from the partnership before we even begin to consider asking a person to be our mentor. The purpose of our mentoring relationships might be to aid us in overcoming a transition or obstacle or to improve in an area where we require additional assistance or direction, but it's up to us to figure it out.

For example, in your workplace, if your manager has urged you to work on being more persuasive in meetings with clients, you should consider which of your coworkers can help you master that skill. Perhaps you have been entrusted with drafting your first marketing strategy so you are looking for pointers from someone else, or you want to apply for a new position or promotion and need some advice on how to move forward in your professional life.

DISCOVERING THE RIGHT MENTOR

Once we have identified the skills and goals we need assistance with, or what questions we have about our work, we should look around our community—including our families, friends, or colleagues—for potential mentors. In the workplace, our mentors do not have to be someone in an executive position, nor do they have to be much older than we. Somebody who is only four to five years our senior might have better insight and provide more useful guidance o since they tend to be more familiar with the daily challenges faced by an individual in our position (Roepe, 2022).

For instance, if you are a programmer seeking to advance into management, you can try to get in touch with your college roommate, with whom you always got along well, and who has been serving as a programming manager for a while. As another example, if you are an entry-level salesperson seeking to specialize in social media, you can consider reaching out to the social media coordinator you have met during a previous internship.

REACHING OUT AND BUILDING A RELATIONSHIP

It is usually preferable to ask a mutual contact to introduce us to a potential mentor if we want to ask somebody we do not know to be our mentor. If we do not have a mutual friend to connect us to that person, it is crucial to first build a common ground before we reach out to them. For instance, we can mention that we attended the same college as them, work in the same field, or are members of the same professional association.

If we have never met a potential mentor, we should tell them what we admire about their work. We have to familiarize ourselves with the work of that person and all the things they have done in their field. Then, we can start praising something about their work. This way, we can show that we have a thoughtful approach when trying to get to know them and ask for their help. We can then begin telling them about ourselves, our work and goals, and the reasons we are contacting them. For example, we can say, "I recently received a promotion to marketing manager, and I want to enhance my readiness for my new position. Would you mind if I ask a few questions regarding how to further develop my skills for the new role?"

MAKING THINGS EASY FOR YOUR MENTOR

We also need to be considerate of our mentors' time by handling the logistics, such as arranging a meeting location or a Skype call, so they can simply show up and provide their guidance. In order to give our mentors time to plan how to best assist us, we should also email them an outline or our list of questions the day prior to our appointment. If our mentors set a one-hour limit for the meeting, we must always be on time and considerate of the time they can spare for us. If we are meeting them in person, we also have to pay for their coffee or food.

LETTING THEM KNOW THAT YOU VALUE THEIR FEEDBACK

If our mentor advises us to take a certain course of action or read a particular book, we should be able to show them that we are implementing their advice by sharing the results of doing so with them via email or at our following meeting. Moreover, we need to follow up on the latter by sharing the lessons we have learned from them. For example, if we read an article that we think our mentor will find useful, we should forward it to them and explain how it connects to a previous discussion that we had.

KEY TAKEAWAYS

- It sounds cliché, but you are the sum of the 5 people you hang around the most. Whether you like it or not, you will be significantly influenced by people who are close to you.
- If you want to change your (work) life for the better, a mentor can be a valuable asset. Having a mentor can benefit you in many ways, from having someone to support your growth, listen to you, and give you constructive feedback to tapping into a source of knowledge, gaining encouragement, helping create new connections, and having a trusted ally.
- Some tips on looking for a mentor and building a relationship with them: knowing what a mentor is, being specific about your goal, discovering the right mentor, reaching out to your mentor, and letting them know that you value their time and feedback.

10

MOTIVATION IS A FEELING THAT COMES AND GOES

"Motivation is fickle. It comes and goes. It is unreliable and when you are counting on motivation to get your goals accomplished – you will likely fall short." – Jocko Willink

MOTIVATION IS NOT A RELIABLE EMOTION

Motivation is one of the buzzwords that is used rather frequently nowadays, specifically when it comes to media advertising. We all have seen various commercials about it, not to mention the countless social media articles and posts that come up on our feeds. Most of the time, in real life, people will say things like, "I am not feeling motivated," or "how do I become more motivated?"

There are days when none of us want to do anything. Perhaps we had a challenging workday, or perhaps we are just feeling lazy and would rather stay in bed all day long. Whatever the cause, it is quite simple to lose motivation these days. From here, we realize that motivation is just an emotion.

Successful people do not believe in motivation as a concept. I personally believe in self-discipline because it always helped me along the way. People who are counting on motivation basically are saying: "I don't feel like doing this. How do I feel like doing this?" And the answer is that you are never going to feel like doing this all the time. This is deeply embedded in human nature.

I remember when I was going to the gym there were days when I simply wasn't motivated to get out of bed even if I enjoyed working out a lot.

If I were to tell you to go skydiving or driving a luxury car every day, there are going to be mornings when you wake up and you just don't feel like doing it, no matter how fun it is. That's life. If you count on motivation, you will never perform against people who act despite how they feel. You must make a decision. Forget about the idea of motivation, throw it away and decide who you are. For me, I decided to be a winner, and I know what it takes to win. To win, I must perform day after day regardless of how I feel. Some days I will enjoy it, some days I will not. However, I don't allow my emotional state to affect my actions. Let's say you are a soccer player and you have a game on March 1st. That day comes and you might feel like you are going to scale and give your best in the game, or you might feel the opposite. But all the tickets are sold, the contracts are signed and nobody cares if you don't feel like doing it. You must be good enough on your worst day to beat your opponent on his best days.

After reading this paragraph take 10 minutes and go look in the mirror and decide who you are going to be. Are you a loser? Because if you are, you can read and watch a variety of motivational speeches, trying to convince yourself to do a bit of work. But in the long run it will be pointless. Or are you a winner?

Motivation is a feeling similar to joy, sadness, anger, or frustration. As with any other emotion, it also can come and go suddenly and for no apparent reason. It is the same as how we can experience moments of happiness, followed by anger. Motivation can change and fade away, as when we may be so utterly irritated at someone initially only to find them funny just moments later; or when we prepare our clothes the night before because we are so excited to hit the gym early in the morning, only to realize that when the alarm goes off at 6 a.m., that is the last place we would like to be, and we just want to stay in bed longer; or when we have prepared for a singing audition months beforehand, but when the day comes to perform, we cannot seem to bring ourselves to attend it anymore. In all of these instances, we simply lose our motivation.

Since we have recognized that motivation is just an emotion, it is not reliable at all. We should not use it as the basis of our decisions and actions in our lives. For example, if you build your marriage with your partner solely around the feeling of passionate attraction, you will be in a lot of trouble when the stress and financial worries set in, and you also have to deal with your children's conflicting schedules. As another example, if you have kids and you base your parenting on never getting annoyed by them, things will not turn out well because raising them can be frustrating and stressful most of the time. You cannot be a good partner or parent if you only rely on motivation when establishing your relationship or raising children.

DISCIPLINE IS FAR MORE IMPORTANT THAN

MOTIVATION

In the end, what distinguishes successful individuals from unsuccessful ones is that they are being disciplined enough to do things even when they are not motivated. It is more crucial to be self-disciplined than to feel motivated, particularly when it comes to long-term objectives. Once we have developed the habit of discipline, we can use it even when we do not feel motivated at all. This is essential because, over time, discipline will enable us to stick to and eventually accomplish our goals even when we do not have any motivation to take action.

Anybody who has ever attempted to accomplish a difficult goal is aware of how important discipline is. When it comes to achieving our goals, discipline is necessary regardless of whether we want to exercise, eat well, or study for a test. The explanation for this is very straightforward: Momentum stems from discipline. The easier anything gets, the more disciplined we are; as a result, we will also build up more momentum (Rothwell, 2022). What was once challenging eventually turns into a habit, and habits are tough to break. Because discipline is essential to bringing about long-lasting change, it is necessary to practice it consistently. Discipline is what enables us to withstand unpleasant feelings, stay on course, and make adjustments in line with our established plans rather than as a result of emotional reactions (Robinson, 2022).

We need to rely on self-discipline because plans are harder to implement than to establish. As an illustration, if you plan to have a healthier lifestyle, you will have to create habits and stick to them– from prepping nutritious homemade meals throughout the week, saying no sugary drinks or alcohol, and eating sufficient protein to working out at the gym 3 times a week, going for a walk, and sleeping enough during the night. You have to do these activities day in and day out in order to make them into habits.

You should not rely on motivation alone because it can disappear in the course of the long journey; rather, you will need to show self-discipline if you want to reach the goal of having a healthier lifestyle. In conclusion, although motivation is an excellent starting point, it is necessary to keep in mind that it will not stay forever. Utilizing motivation to make it through the day can be an up-and-down roller coaster for us.

Moreover, even though maintaining discipline through daily routines and habits may appear boring, we are actually making progress every day. When we practice self-discipline in one area of our lives, it naturally extends and moves to other aspects of our lives, which will surprise us.

HOW TO KEEP GOING EVEN WHEN YOU ARE NOT MOTIVATED

Everybody experiences days when they lack the motivation to function or even get out of bed. It is common to experience these feelings occasionally. It is possible that we are under stress because of a task at our workplace or a personal problem. Whatever the cause, it is important to keep in mind that these emotions are temporary because they will eventually pass. When we are lacking motivation, we can try these things to get through the day:

- Taking a break: When we feel down or unmotivated, we need to leave what we are doing where we are at. We can try going for a stroll, turning on some music, opening a book, or cooking our favorite meal. Whatever activity we choose, we need to ensure that they can calm us down. We must set aside some time for rest and rejuvenation. Once our minds are relaxed, we will be able to focus on what things are necessary to finish.

- Transcending our environment: Occasionally, a change of setting is all that is required. If we work from home, we can consider visiting a coffee shop or a public park. Changing our surroundings can help our creativity take off if we are stuck. If we work from the office, we can declutter our workspace or even decorate it with all the things we like. When we feel happy with our environment, it will be much easier to work through our tasks.

- Talking to someone: When we are feeling low, talking to someone can be therapeutic and beneficial. This can facilitate the processing of our emotions and the creation of an action plan that we need. By speaking with a friend or a member of our family, we will also feel supported and cared for. Our loved ones may provide us with solutions or advice for our issues, as well as with emotional support.

- Taking action: Oftentimes taking action is the greatest way to break out of a block. We can try to start that task we have been putting off, or take a stroll around our neighborhood. Doing something, no matter how small or trivial, may be able to help us get out of our mind block.

- Using Inspiration: Inspiration is stronger than motivation. We are inspired to take action when we encounter something which inspires us. For example, when we witness someone else achieve their dream of establishing their own company, we are inspired to do the same. This is why it is essential to surround ourselves with people who can inspire us and look for new inspiration as well.

Once we become more self-disciplined, we will begin to see the outcomes we seek. However, we must be cautious to limit the number of these strenuous days to avoid feeling burnt out. By following the steps outlined above, we can keep working toward our goals productively.

KEY TAKEAWAYS

- Discipline accounts for 99% of the job we are doing, and motivation for the remaining 1%. This is why this chapter is teaching us not to rely solely on motivation.
- As motivation comes and goes, we should focus our energy on developing our self-discipline instead.
- Successful people already realize how important it is to keep going even when they do not feel motivated, and that is because they have self-discipline.
- Our emotions are temporary. When you are feeling low, keep in mind these four hacks: taking a break, transcending your environment, talking to someone, taking action, and using inspiration.

11

BUILDING HEALTHY HABITS

"Extraordinary habits are what allow people to perform at an elite level."- Ed Mylett

STARTING SMALL WITH ATOMIC HABITS

Do you want to improve the quality of your life and become more self-disciplined? That is fantastic, but you cannot accomplish this overnight. There is a process to follow, and we all must be prepared to put in the necessary effort. It is possible to build productive and healthy habits, and we need to start small for that.

James Clear, an expert on long-term habit development, asserts in his book *Atomic Habits* that by making minor alterations to our daily routines, we may be able to create good habits and also break negative ones (Goeke, 2018). In another sense, if we learn a small habit, or atomic habit, and practice it consistently, we can make incredible improvements in our lives. Atomic habits are small, recurring behaviors that are easy to pick up and maintain yet have a significant impact on how we conduct our daily lives (Clear, 2018).

TAKING IT STEP BY STEP

We should choose a new habit that is so small and simple that it does not need much effort to get done. One percent gains mount up quite quickly as well as one percent drops. Instead of attempting something extraordinary right away, we should start small and get better over time (Clear, 2022). For example, if we want to start doing sit-ups, we can try 5 on the first day, 6 on the second, 7 on the third, and so on. Likewise, if you want to build up your meditation to 30 minutes, start by dividing it into two stages of 15 minutes each. We have to make a habit simple enough so that we can do it easily without putting much effort in the beginning. Every habit needs to be manageable in order to keep momentum and make the action as simple as possible to carry out

(Clear, 2022). Our motivation and willpower will grow along the journey. As a result, it will be easier for us to maintain our habits in the long run.

GETTING BACK ON TRACK

Like everybody else in this world, top performers can make mistakes and stray from their intended path. The difference is that they get back on track as soon as they can. Although we should not expect to fail, we still have to prepare for those things that can get us off track. What are some common emergencies that can arise? How are we going to move past these problems? Or, at the very least, how can we efficiently recover from them and steady the course? Remember, we just have to be consistent, not perfect.

BUILDING HEALTHY HABITS IN 4 EASY STEPS

The fundamental steps that make up the habit-forming process are cue, craving, response, and reward. We can better comprehend what a habit is, how it functions, and how to change it by splitting it into these fundamental elements. Clear believes that the environment acts as an invisible force to mold human behavior when it comes to habits (Goeke, 2018). Therefore, the first action in establishing any habit is to always use a cue. Though it might not always be external, the majority of the time it will be. Each specific step of the four-stage pattern is described below.

- Cue: a clue that points to a potential reward, such as the aroma of baking cookies or a completely dark room that will shortly be lit up.
- Craving: the motivation to make a transformation so that we can reap the benefits, like tasting the cookie's deliciousness after baking them or being able to see when we turn on the light.
- Response: taking whatever steps or actions are necessary to reach the reward.

- Reward: the positive feeling we have as a result of the changes and the knowledge of whether to repeat it or not.

USING THE FOUR LAWS OF BEHAVIOR CHANGE

These four steps can be combined to create a useful framework that can create healthy habits and get rid of undesirable ones. Clear refers to this framework as the "four laws of behavior change" (Clear, 2018). Here they are, along with some suggestions for how to utilize them to foster positive behavior.

- Making it obvious: If we want to lead a healthier life, we should put the fruits we buy from the grocery store on display rather than hiding them at the back of our fridge.
- Making it attractive: When we are shopping for fruits, we should choose the ones that we truly enjoy eating so that when we see them, we will actually want to eat some.
- Making it easy: We should not create any unnecessary steps by choosing fruits that are more difficult to peel. For example, instead of choosing a watermelon, we can get a banana or an apple since they are very easy to eat.
- Making it satisfying: If we like the fruits we have bought, we will enjoy eating them and feel much healthier as a result.

These behaviors can support a variety of healthy habits, such as exercising, working on a side business, investing extra time with family, and so on. For a bad habit, on the other hand, we need to do the reverse. We should make it invisible, unattractive, difficult, and unsatisfying (Clear, 2018). We may, for instance, hide our cigarettes, impose fines, eliminate all lighters, and restrict our smoking time only outside, during cold nights.

HEALTHY HABITS YOU CAN BUILD NO MATTER WHAT YOUR GOALS ARE

NOT CHECKING YOUR PHONE FIRST THING IN THE MORNING

After waking up in the morning, we must try to keep our phone away and not check it for the first 30 minutes. We should instead use that time to accomplish something we deem more important. Some of these activities can be meditating for 15 minutes, taking a cold shower, writing down our goals, visualizing our future goals, and so forth. In addition, if not checking your phone in the morning turns out to be too much of a challenge, you can leave it in your car the night before.

KEEPING THE PROMISES YOU MAKE TO YOURSELF

Everyone who has experienced having a promise broken knows how frustrating or disappointing it can be. While keeping our promises to other people is a crucial component of a relationship, honoring our promise to ourselves is just as vital, if not more so. Every time we keep our word to ourselves, we demonstrate that we are reliable, that we honor our promise, and that we can depend on ourselves to meet our responsibilities. As a result, it will increase our self-confidence and self-esteem.

FOCUSING ON THE GOAL, NOT THE COST

We need to stop focusing on the cost and effort required to obtain our desired results and goals. For instance, we may need to purchase a course to help us expand our business or pick up a new talent, but we are unsure what to do when we see the price tag. We need to put an end to the negotiation; if the course can alter our lives for the better, it is definitely worthwhile. If we keep our eyes on the price tag only, we will inevitably give up on reaching our goals. Even if those around us tell us it will cost too much, we must fully commit to what we wish to accomplish.

GETTING LASER FOCUS

Procrastination is easily overcome if we can cultivate sufficient concentration skills. The ability to dedicate all of our mental energy to an activity we are actively prioritizing is known as laser focus. This allows us to shut out distractions, put all of our tempting, extraneous thoughts aside, and maintain the drive required to achieve our goals. One focusing strategy involves not just visualizing our dreams but also actively observing and learning from people who have reached theirs. Let's say you want to be a fitness model or influencer. You might attend sessions on bodybuilding, or follow influencers on social media to see what content they create and how. Or, if you're struggling to save the money you need to afford your dream car, you can go to a car dealership to test drive that car once in a while to see what it feels like to drive it.

OVERCOMING YOUR FEARS AND TAKING RISKS

We should never let fear dictate who we are or the things we are going to do. It is possible that we develop fears that are unnecessary, such as anxiety about public speaking. We can be hindered from moving forward in our work or taking part in activities, like making a toast at our closest friend's wedding due to our fear of public speaking. We need to take one little step at a time while facing our fears. When we are not ready, moving too quickly or doing something dangerous can backfire. We have to feel the fear first and keep moving forward slowly. It is okay to feel a little anxious.

By the same token, our opportunities are increased when we take risks and try new things. We will never get the chance to reach our goals if we insist on total safety and assurance. It is an uncomfortable truth, but in order to do anything worthwhile, we must act and venture into unfamiliar territory. Planning is the first step toward taking a risk. It involves searching within and asking yourself, "what do I really want?" Once we can answer this question, we should then make a strategy to get there and truly commit to turning it into a reality. When it involves achievement and goal-setting, taking reasonable, measured risks may be a game-changer.

WRITING DOWN ALL THE GOOD THINGS IN YOUR LIFE

We inevitably transform into optimistic people when we concentrate on all the positive aspects of our lives. Simply listing the good things that happen to us each day, small and big, for which we are grateful will boost our optimism and make us happier. Merely thinking about them will not help us make them come true; we need to write them down and act on them. We might encounter challenging circumstances on some days, or there might be roadblocks in our path, but every day has some positive aspects to it. For example, we can write down that we are grateful for our family, the food we eat, the water we drink, and so on.

COMMITTING TO CONTINUOUS IMPROVEMENT

The continuous improvement method emphasizes producing small progress over time rather than making significant improvements all at once. Improvements must be continually worked on in order to be maintained. Our pursuit of personal improvement never ends, and when we embrace it, we are much less likely to give up since we are constantly looking for the next challenge. For example, if you have a business, you will work on expanding it as much as you can by regularly developing and implementing better business ideas.

BEING HUMBLE

As already stated, we need to stay open to learning from more experienced people who have achieved the same goals we are pursuing so that we can follow in their steps. By the same token, we should stay humble because overconfidence can lead to arrogance. Take Koby Bryant, for example. Even when he became one of the best basketball players of all time, he still looked up to

Michael Jordan, his coach, and others, who were able to teach him more things.

KEY TAKEAWAYS

- We all know how easy it is to fall into bad habits that we cannot get out of. Hence the need to establish new healthy habits in order to lead a better life.
- If we plan on forming a new habit, we should start with something small, an "atomic habit," as James Clear explains in his book. Nothing will stick to us if we start big because we can get overwhelmed and stop in the middle of the journey.
- According to Clear, there are also 4 steps in building healthy habits: cue, craving, response, and reward.
- No matter what your goals are, here are some healthy habits you should cultivate: not checking your phone first thing in the morning, keeping the promises you make to yourself, getting laser focus, overcoming your fears and taking risks, focusing on the results and ignoring the costs, writing down all the good things in your life, committing to continuous improvement, and not being arrogant.

12

ELIMINATING EXCUSES

"I attribute my success to this: - I never gave or took an excuse."-
Florence Nightingale

Making excuses is a typical human reaction because, as social creatures, we worry about what other people think of us and want to fit in. We create excuses and avoid responsibilities instead of dealing with difficult situations and emotions. Making excuses can make people feel relieved only for a moment since they have protected themselves from some discomfort (Robbins, 2022). However, over time, they might feel unfulfilled, anxious, or depressed because of this.

The hardest part about making excuses is that they frequently contain a bit of truth. Imagine that due to a car wreck, two roads were closed, causing you to miss the meeting that morning. It also may be true that on the evening your essay was due, the internet went out all of a sudden. Saying that you could have become more successful had your family supported you more sounds like a reasonable statement. There are lots of reasonable explanations for why success is very difficult to achieve. However, wouldn't you want to exchange each excuse for the chance to succeed? That is the problem with excuses. Despite how good they are, they show us that we did not do the things we set out to do. We must learn how to stop making them if we want to become self-disciplined and reach success later on.

WHY DO YOU MAKE EXCUSES?

We can make sure that we will always be in charge of our lives by understanding how to avoid making excuses. People typically make up excuses because they do not like a certain result in their lives. This might concern their health, income, family life, or careers. We have two options when asked why our lives are not the way we want them to be: We can give an excuse or we can take responsibility. Many people make the error of blaming their shortcomings on uncontrollable external factors for what happens. Although they may appear insignificant, excuses may seriously hinder our efforts to live the life of our dreams.

Let's say that your goal is to lose 30 pounds of weight in 3 months. At the end of 3 months, you weighed yourself and found out that you had only lost 10 pounds. As you consider what could have gone wrong, you think about all the cheat meals you had eaten when you should have been dieting. Moreover, you also remember the time you skipped your gym workout because you felt like you were too exhausted or busy. Instead of making excuses and actually accepting responsibility here, you give yourself the chance to do better in the future.

For example, if you recognize that you have failed to accomplish your weight loss target because you did not stick to the plan, what you can do is figure out how to follow it better. If you had followed all the steps in the plan and still did not reach the goal, then you should reconsider the plan you made. In this case, you might see if your plan was unrealistic for you to follow at the moment. You have two options in this scenario: You may either change your goal entirely or lengthen the time you give yourself to complete it. In either situation, you are fully aware of how to bring about the changes you desire in your life.

When we blame our failures on a scenario or situation that we cannot control, we will find ourselves waiting for the world to deliver us the life we want. Those who are aware of how excuses can hinder their chances of success will welcome the chance to accept responsibility for the things that happen in their lives (Griggs, 2022).

HOW TO ELIMINATE EXCUSES

UNDERSTANDING THE NEED TO LEAVE YOUR COMFORT ZONE

If we wish to eliminate excuses from our lives, we need to concentrate on the reasons why we desire a better life for ourselves. When hesitations enter our heads, we will begin to find excuses to maintain things just the way they are. Our desire to carry on is the furthest thing from our minds when we are in this situation.

Therefore, whatever excuse we may come up with is an effort to return to our comfortable environments. Yet the most dangerous thing about our comfort zone is precisely that it may feel so comfortable because of all the routines that we have gotten used to. The issue with keeping ourselves in our comfort zone is that it limits our ability to take risks and try new things, stretch our interests, and experience the improvements we wish to make.

AVOIDING OTHER EXCUSERS

When we begin moving outside our comfort zone, we will realize that a lot of people in our lives are also making excuses. If we analyze the conversations with them, we will find out how many times we would complain and make excuses for everything. Instead of engaging in these pointless conversations, we should spend our time doing something that is actually important.

Like us, these people do not know that they are making excuses; everybody must come to this conclusion on their own first before they can transform themselves. For example, when we talk to these people, we need to start a fresh conversation and be the ones to shift the topic so that we do not complain and whine about the things we can actually change. Eliminating our excuses will probably inspire others we care about to follow the same path.

KEEPING IN MIND YOUR REASONS TO PERSEVERE

We need to remind ourselves of our goals and work passionately toward them at all times if we want to step outside of our comfort zone and avoid making excuses. Each time we give in to excuses, we give ourselves a reason for accepting our lives as they are. There will constantly be an excuse to put something off until later, but we cannot let ourselves do this all the time. We have to ask ourselves, "How do I see myself changing if I achieve my goal? Will I be in a better position to look after my family and advocate for issues I care about?" No matter the reason, we have to realize that making excuses will prevent us from achieving our life goals.

NOT BLAMING OTHERS

People who make excuses frequently blame others for their situations. This way of thinking shows that we lack control over our life and rely too much on external factors rather than our efforts to influence them. As opposed to taking an active role in shaping our destiny, it makes us victims of life.

We all know a person who consistently finds someone else to blame for their problems and who is unhappy in many areas of their life. Maybe you are that person? Perhaps you like making excuses, whether you are blaming the place in which you live, your parents, or the condition of the world today. Many successful people have experienced hardships in their lives; some grew up poor, while others were forced to flee their homes, but they managed to rise above these adversities. It is essential that we take charge of our lives and understand that we are responsible for our future. In order to realize we are not alone and we are not victims, we can read and draw inspiration from others' success stories.

CONQUERING YOUR FEAR OF FAILURE

The ability to quit making excuses enables us to accept the fact that mistakes will occasionally happen. Most people make excuses for their inaction because they are afraid of failing. It is

115

challenging to take a leap into doing a new thing. We find ourselves overwhelmed with thoughts about the worst-case scenario because we want to be safe (Brady, 2022).

As an example, if you are looking for a new job or to launch a business, your mind might be worried that you will lose your steady income. Your mind immediately starts coming up with all the reasons you need to stay at your current job when you begin to see yourself leaving. The promotion you did not get may make you question whether you ever wanted it. You might even ask yourself if dealing with more work and responsibilities is really worth all the hassle. You begin to consider yourself fortunate that you were not promoted once you realize that the higher income is not worth the stress of extra work.

You have come up with a number of excuses for keeping things as they are for a short period of time. The answer to all of these questions will be the same once you accept responsibility for the outcomes in your life. Even though you might not be certain of what is ahead of you, you are confident in your ability to handle the challenge. No matter the obstacle, you are confident that you will acquire the abilities required to overcome it.

KEY TAKEAWAYS

- As obvious as it may seem, we cannot allow ourselves to think that life is something that just happens to us because a lot of things in our lives are under our control.
- The first move in improving our lives is understanding how to quit making excuses since we are the ones who create them.
- An incredible thing will happen when we accept responsibility for our lives: We will begin to explore strategies to quit making excuses and have consistent self-discipline as a result.
- Tips on eliminating excuses: understanding the need to leave your comfort zone, avoiding other excusers, keeping in mind your reasons to persevere, not blaming others, and overcoming your fear of failure.

13

DOING THE THINGS UNSUCCESSFUL PEOPLE WON'T DO

"If you can get through doing things that you hate to do, on the other side is greatness."- David Goggins

This sounds like an old cliché but it is true; everybody wants to be successful, yet only a limited number of people actually get to the point where they can enjoy both their professional and personal achievements, no matter how small. How do we stay away from the dangers and bad habits that most unsuccessful people engage in? We can do this by doing all the things that unsuccessful people won't do. Precisely because it is so easy to pass up opportunities, we need to learn how to take more action in our lives because successful people are more willing to move forward. Here are some of the activities that successful people need to do.

TAKING MORE RISKS

Successful people have a very different attitude than unsuccessful ones, as can be seen by observing their behavior. A willingness to take risks is one of the key traits separating successful and unsuccessful people. Let's say you are interested in the stock market and want to invest someday. However, you are scared that you may not be able to get any profit if your calculation is wrong. Successful people will try their best to learn all about the stock market and take the risk of losing money. Even if they fail the first time, they can still learn from their mistakes and try another time.

As pointed out in the previous chapter, doing only what feels comfortable will not benefit us in the long run. We cannot avoid taking risks in life, so we might as well embrace challenges, thinking of them as opportunities to practice self-discipline and thereby to learn and grow. If we can accomplish a difficult task, we will gain the confidence necessary to take on others.

DEALING WITH A CHALLENGE, NO MATTER HOW DIFFICULT

Our brains thrive on a challenge, but only when it is presented in the correct way. If something is too simple, our minds become bored and switch to a different thing. If it is too difficult, we instantly lose interest and shift to something else. Taking on challenges involves more than just being willing to have uncomfortable discussions, recognizing failure as a necessary part of the process, and remaining true to our vision. Additionally, it involves continually repeating the steps, despite how boring and challenging they may get.

For example, talent alone is insufficient in order to become a great runner. Having the right body is also not enough here. A runner must increase their endurance over longer distances by constantly performing a ton of exercises even though these might feel like an endless stretch of roads in the beginning. A great runner is created over time because they are willing to go through difficult and boring challenges.

FOCUSING ON YOUR GOALS DAILY

Envisaging success is another trait of successful people. For example, Vanessa has been writing down her goals as soon as she wakes up every morning for years. In her experience, no matter how ridiculous the goal is, if she can maintain her concentration, she will succeed in achieving it. She believes that when she has a clear sense of her unfulfilled goals, they are more likely to become a reality. We can try to do the same as Vanessa and focus on our success by making it clear in our minds. Unsuccessful people do not seem to be in control of what they concentrate on; they tend to let anything wander into their thoughts and environments. Despite how big or insignificant our goals are, we all have the chance to accomplish them every day.

GETTING UP EARLY

A lot of unsuccessful people refuse to get up early in the morning or even get out of bed. In order to have more time to reach our goals, we need to push ourselves to wake up early. Approximately half of the self-made billionaires rose a minimum of three hours before their workday officially began (Ward, 2017). Most of them work on personal projects in their spare time, create plans for their days, or schedule workouts. Why do they do this, and why do we need to follow this habit? We will be able to take back control of our lives by waking at 5 a.m. and tackling the top three tasks we want to complete for the day. As a result, we feel more confident in what we do and take charge of our lives too.

SPENDING TIME WITH THOSE WHO INSPIRE YOU

As mentioned in the previous chapters, spending time with those who inspire you is a must if you want to be successful. We are only as successful as the people we hang around with the most. We should not worry if we do not yet have highly driven individuals in our personal network. A lot of successful businessmen spend their free time volunteering, which is a fantastic way to connect with other inspiring, driven people (Imafidon, 2022). Moreover, we can also join communities for people with similar hobbies or careers and then communicate with them in order to establish relationships. We also have to choose whom we spend time with carefully. Additionally, successful people make it a point to limit their contact with toxic and negative individuals.

BEING CAUTIOUSLY OPTIMISTIC

Wherever possible, successful people focus their attention on the positive side of things, yet not blindly. Having an optimistic attitude enables us to see possibilities and alternatives that we otherwise would not, while accepting that we cannot always predict or control the future. Still, we must have faith that we can cope with the obstacles that we are likely to encounter along the way; otherwise, we will either give up before the trip is over or fail in our journey.

Hence the need to become good thinkers so that we can find solutions whenever something negative comes our way. One of the most important tools for a successful individual is critical thinking. Problem-solvers are constantly coming up with new ideas and looking toward the future. For example, if you have just been laid off, what are you going to do? Keeping a positive attitude does not mean that you can just sit around and wait for opportunities to come to you. You will need to take action. Perhaps this is your chance to implement the business idea that you have been putting off. You have to believe that there are opportunities out there and be willing to go after them.

READING BOOKS

Unsuccessful people do not care about gaining new knowledge and understanding others' perspectives. If we want to become successful, we need to expand our horizons by reading books in a variety of genres, such as biography, history, self-help, and fiction. Reading for pleasure can also advance our professional careers (Ward, 2016). Warren Buffet, a renowned investor and self-made billionaire, claims that reading is his most important habit (Ward, 2017). After reading a book, we also need to apply the knowledge we have learned in real life, or it will be useless. For instance, if you have just read a self-help book on quitting procrastination, you have to start practicing the tips mentioned there. If not, you will never be able to quit procrastination as you intend to do.

SETTING BOUNDARIES

Successful people set not only specific goals but also clear boundaries in pursuit of those goals. Thus, if you work in the business world, you need to realize that not all business ideas are good, and not all partnerships are advantageous for you. Successful businessmen are aware that they cannot accept every proposal or collaborate with everybody. Oftentimes we have to put our needs first, taking a little break and saying no to more hours of work. It might feel like we are not working hard enough, but we all need time for ourselves and our loved ones.

KEY TAKEAWAYS

- What sets successful and unsuccessful people apart? It is all about taking action and moving forward with our plans, in spite of obstacles or fear of failure.
- A successful person demonstrates the persistence and commitment necessary for success. They practice self-discipline, are determined to succeed, and put in a lot of effort. People who are successful are also tireless in these pursuits.
- Things unsuccessful people won't do: taking more risks, dealing with a challenge, focusing on goals daily, getting up early, spending time with those who inspire you, being cautiously optimistic, reading books, and setting boundaries.

14

PLANNING YOUR DAY BY CREATING A TO-DO LIST

"Make a damn schedule."- Jordan Person

It is often said that the best, if not the only way, to control the future is to plan for it. Establishing a schedule of activities we wish to complete each day allows us to stay productive and organized. When people implement such plans into their routines, the majority of them notice significant advantages in their lives. Planning your day is best done the night prior or first thing each morning. You can choose the time depending on what works for you best.

THE ADVANTAGES OF PLANNING YOUR DAY

FREEING UP MORE TIME IN YOUR DAY

Most people do not even consider planning their days because they genuinely believe that doing so will limit their freedom. They claim that planning their time reduces their flexibility. They believe it will drain the day's excitement and ruin their "young, wild, and free" mentality (Canelas, 2021). Consider, however, consider the possibility–and consequences–of a missed deadline or a forgotten task.

We outline our future success when we start each day with a clear plan. We possess the freedom to set aside time for work, fun, extracurricular activities, and side hobbies. We are able to create the freedom we desire instead of waiting for it to come. If we feel like working additional hours on particular days, we can plan those times in advance. Alternatively, if we feel like staying away from work, either to relax or spend time with the family, we can take a day off as well.

In my case, once I started doing daily planning, I had the opportunity to read books, keep a journal, travel, spend quality time with my loved ones, and learn new things. It was not a matter of having the time anymore; it was a matter of making the time.

BECOMING MORE PRODUCTIVE AND LESS BUSY

As an example, Matthew has never tried to plan his working days before, and as a result, he never knows where to start doing his tasks. When his work is not busy and there is not much to do, he is fine. However, when his boss gives him a lot of tasks at once, he becomes very overwhelmed and ends up wasting time on unnecessary things–until one day, when his coworker suggests that he starts planning his day. Matthew finally does so and after a while, he realizes that everything becomes so organized that he is no longer wasting time on pointless activities. While time-filler activities occupy our time for their own sake without producing anything, time-feeder activities fill it with progress and accomplishments (Canelas, 2022). Planning our day also increases our productive hours as opposed to merely working more hours. When we make a plan for the day, we intentionally choose whether to be busy or productive with our time. We can start by figuring out what contributes most to the things we are working on, followed by developing a plan, putting it into action, and managing our productive time.

FEELING MORE EXCITED

When we plan our day, we will feel more excited to go through it. We are all aware of the excitement that comes with organizing our next vacations; this excitement typically matches that of actually going on holiday. The process of picturing and writing out a plan offers us something to hold on to, even when that thing is repetitive. For example, you have a blog where you like to write and post different articles about celebrities. Choosing whom to focus on next adds to the excitement of writing your posts. You know you do this every week, but because your focus varies, you will still be enthusiastic about this activity each time.

ENHANCING YOUR FOCUS

We all have been through those awful mornings when nothing makes sense. We are unsure of our responsibilities, so we lack focus as we move from task to task since there is no plan to guide us. Those days, which I refer to as trashy days, have that feeling. On the other hand, when our day is planned out in advance, we are less inclined to fall victim to distractions or lose time wondering what we need to do next. With a plan in place, it will be easier to navigate the day, without doubts or uncertainties. A plan gives us direction and purpose, focusing our attention on our long-term goal and the tasks at hand.

GETTING MORE QUALITY SLEEP

Oskar has been having a hard time sleeping during the night. He has a big project coming up at work and he is not sure where to begin or how to do it well. He feels that the project is so overwhelming that it has taken over his sleeping hours. An overactive mind full of racing thoughts is one of the most typical causes of insomnia. It is difficult to get quality sleep and stay asleep if we cannot stop thinking and worrying. All humans experience fears and anxieties about the future, but there are ways to minimize the stress of such thoughts. While writing them down can be therapeutic, it is planning that genuinely frees us from these worries. Making plans for the following day in the evening can help us get better quality sleep and feel more relaxed (Marvin, 2022).

MEETING YOUR DEADLINES BY SCAFFOLDING YOUR PROJECTS

We can more easily meet deadlines when we plan our day. Doing so may help us break our big projects into small tasks so that we can establish a timeline to make sure that we complete them by a specific time or date. We will also be able to keep track of important deadlines and remind ourselves about them by reviewing the schedule every day. This practice also enables us to modify our schedule as we go. For example, your team is tasked by your company to create a new logo for them. This is a big project, so when you plan your day, you need to divide it into manageable tasks. You can say that on the first day you will brainstorm ideas with your team, on the second day you will create the design, and so forth.

HAVING LESS STRESS

Lack of organization causes high levels of stress that are detrimental to our health, both physical and mental, thus preventing us from producing quality work. We can all draw up a list of goals, activities, and tasks that are realistic and thus attainable. However, without a guide to follow, we will probably struggle or simply give up. One advantage of planning our day is stress reduction. For example, if you want to quit your current job and get a new one, the steps to get a new job would be to update your resume, search for job vacancies, and apply to different companies. Once you get accepted to a new job, your next step would be to submit your resignation letter, wait for the two-week notice, and then finally start your new job. When we have outlined the ways to get there, we will worry less about the outcome. Even though the plan might not always yield the best or desired outcome, at least we have a strong starting point. With a set strategy, we will be able to accomplish far more with a lot less stress.

HOW TO CREATE A TO-DO LIST

A to-do list is a collection of things that we need to get done within a certain time frame, such as a day, a week, or even only a part of the day (Kiander, 2022). These lists, which frequently contain manageable activities, encourage productivity and prevent procrastination. There are often two styles for to-do lists: either we place the most important things at the top and the least significant ones at the bottom, or we arrange the activities so that they progress from easily achievable to more difficult. Staying organized and setting reminders to become much easier as a result. So how do you create a to-do list? Here are some steps.

Firstly, you should not create the list in a hurry; instead, take your time, giving yourself at least 15 minutes. If necessary, find a quiet place, whether inside or outside our house, so that you can carefully analyze your tasks before adding them to the to-do list. Secondly, write tasks and not goals. The latter should be on a different list. While tasks might help us move toward our goals, goals are bigger objectives that we cannot accomplish in a single day. For example, if your goal is to learn to speak Spanish, you can break it down into a task by writing "see a movie in Spanish" or "read a Spanish book for 20 minutes."

Thirdly, keep your to-do lists brief so that they can be read quickly to determine what needs to be done next. To this end, look for keywords identifying the relevant tasks. If let's say, you intend to clean up your house, you might jot down something short, like "clean house," rather than a long sentence.

Lastly, prioritize your tasks. It is difficult to know the exact number of tasks we should have on our daily to-do list. Depending on our circumstances, anything between 5 and 10 activities should be sufficient for the day. We should recognize that some tasks can be completed quickly, making it simpler to add more and organize our activities on certain days.

TIPS ON PLANNING YOUR DAY

When attempting to create a plan for our day, there are several things we can do to increase its effectiveness. Here are some tips we can utilize in order to create a good to-do list.

USING A PLANNING TOOL

Organizing our day will be much easier with a planning tool. An actual paper planner, a smartphone app, or software applications are all examples of planning tools. If we create our to-do list in the same place each day, we will always know where to find it. It will also become easier to review past plans to include relevant information for that day. Pick a planning tool that fits your needs the best.

CREATING CATEGORIES FOR YOUR TASKS

We can try categorizing our tasks for better organization within our daily agenda. We may analyze our most frequent tasks, then categorize them into groups based on similarity. For instance, we can create sections for meetings, calls and emails, work projects, and personal matters. We will be able to see more clearly the kind of tasks we have for the day by establishing categories.

LEAVING SPACE FOR ADJUSTMENTS

It can be helpful to create your to-do list while keeping in mind that changes might be necessary due to unforeseen circumstances. For instance, if we know that we have a task that needs to be completed at the end of the day, we can try to get it done one hour earlier. This will give us the time to complete our tasks before something unpredictable occurs during the day. In order to create this extra time in our daily plan, we can either allow ourselves more time than we estimate for more difficult tasks or set aside some free time.

UPDATING YOUR PLANS DURING THE DAY

It would be ideal if we were able to stick to our schedule every day exactly as it was intended. However, unpredictable circumstances sometimes may occur, and they occasionally make finishing a task take longer or shorter than expected. It is a good idea to modify our daily schedule during the day to get the most out of it. For instance, if we complete a task early, we can reschedule, or even get started on, other tasks that were set for later in the day.

REVIEWING YOUR PROGRESS AT THE END OF EACH DAY

Make a habit of reviewing your to-do list each night, looking very closely for any tasks you were not able to finish that day. These things can be included in your plan for the following day to help you remember to finish them. check whether certain tasks took you longer or shorter than intended when reviewing your progress for the day so that you can make future plans that are more accurate. For instance, if you find that you have often finished a task ahead of schedule, you can allocate less time when you need to do that task again.

KEY TAKEAWAYS

- When we have so many things to do, it can get very overwhelming when we are not sure where to start doing our tasks. Hence it is very important for us to plan our day by creating a to-do list.
- Creating a to-do list will enable us to get more freedom in our day, become more productive and less busy, feel more excited, enhance our focus, get more quality sleep, meet our deadlines, scaffold big projects, and have less stress.
- In order to get through our day much more easier, we need to take our time in making the to-do list, putting tasks, not goals on it, setting our priorities, and leaving room for the unexpected.
- Some important tips for planning our day so that it can be effective and we can turn it into our new habit are as follows: using a planning tool, creating categories for our tasks, updating our plans during the day, and reviewing our progress at the end of each day.

15

FINDING AN ACCOUNTABILITY PARTNER

"Your accountability partner keeps you on track and moving forward in all aspects of your development."- Mike Staver

WHAT EXACTLY IS ACCOUNTABILITY AND WHY DOES IT MATTER?

Taking accountability means recognizing that you are the only one who is responsible for your success. It involves taking responsibility for your actions and for pursuing attainable, realistic goals for success. Accountability is the measurement we use to assess every action's influence and effect as well as determine whether it will move us closer or further away from our end goals (Finkelstein, 2020). Simply put, accountability means doing what you say you will do. For example, let's imagine that you say you are going to open up a new business. If you hold yourself accountable for that decision, you will definitely start doing the things needed to launch the business idea.

Accountability is crucial in every undertaking. It ensures that we thoroughly analyze our decisions and weigh the results of each action against the goal we intend to accomplish. Accountability assists us not just in overcoming uncertainty but also in maintaining our motivation and overcoming negative views, feelings, and behavior patterns (Braun, 2022). However, if we often struggle to hold ourselves accountable or if we are unsure of how to begin practicing self-accountability, then we might benefit from having an accountability partner to guide us. Keep in mind that having an accountability partner is different from having a mentor.

WHY DO YOU NEED AN ACCOUNTABILITY PARTNER?

We have already emphasized, in Chapter 9, the benefits of surrounding yourself with successful people, but the ideal companion for your self-exploratory journey toward accountability is an accountability partner (Finkelstein, 2022). That person might be a supportive friend, family member, colleague, or even an outsider—a knowledgeable and caring individual who can help you maintain focus and motivation while you're working toward your goals, and who can also help you identify your strengths and weaknesses. The more specific benefits of having an accountability partner are described below.

OFFERING GUIDANCE AND ADVICE

Our accountability partners can help us evaluate our success because they are unbiased witnesses of our journey. They can also guide us in determining our strengths and shortcomings. They will identify areas that need more focus and attention so that we can improve them. For instance, if you desire to get promoted at your workplace, an accountability partner can help tell you which skills to improve or which habits to get rid of. If you have a bad habit of showing up late to work, your accountability partner will hold you accountable for this behavior and ask you to change in order to get the promotion. In doing so, we will be able to gain a deeper insight into our behavior, ideas, and feelings.

HELPING YOU STAY ON TRACK

An accountability partner, who genuinely cares about our goals and supports them, might assist in helping us identify the moments when we start to lose focus. By reminding us of the advantages of reaching our goals, they can help us to get back on track and serve as a constant source of inspiration and encouragement. They also help in keeping our energy and willpower—indeed, our discipline—strong.

Let's say you plan to expand your business to another country, but you come up against so many hurdles that you end up putting it off. In this scenario, an accountability partner would be there to remind you about your goal and encourage you to stick to your plan. Telling yourself "I have plenty of time" or "I can do it whenever I want" will never help you grow. This kind of attitude will never be enough in getting you to follow through on your goals because you will keep thinking that there is always tomorrow to take action.

HELPING YOU PUSH YOUR LIMITS

We will be able to test our skills and identify areas where more substantial improvement can be made with the assistance of an accountability partner. We can then aim higher and set more important goals. For example, you are not sure that you can get promoted at work because you think that your public speaking and leadership abilities are lacking. An accountability partner will be the one to push you to improve these skills so that you can get a better position at work. In general, accountability allows us to discover and make the most of our abilities, but sometimes we all need a nudge in the right direction or a reminder of what we are truly capable of. We cannot always get to a better place if we go and do it alone. The journey becomes a more meaningful experience with others by our side.

SHARING IN OUR HAPPINESS AND SUCCESS

The ideal person with whom to share our happiness and success in our accomplishments is an accountability partner. Our accountability partners can help us gain a fresh perspective on all the goals we have achieved and set new ones, thus boosting our self-confidence and motivating us to excel at what we are doing. When we collaborate and build on each other's strengths while recognizing our shortcomings, we may help each other succeed and grow. Once we have achieved our goals, we can then share our happiness and victories with them.

HOW TO DISCOVER THE RIGHT ACCOUNTABILITY PARTNER

Choosing and discovering an accountability partner can be challenging because we are looking for someone who

- is pursuing goals that match with yours
- assumes responsibility for those goals as well
- is at ease discussing sensitive information with you and you with them
- uses similar methods of communication, such as email, text messages, phone calls, video calls, or in-person.

Finding someone who meets our criteria can seem like finding a needle in a haystack, but we can increase our chances if we make a conscious effort to do so.

MAKING A LIST

The first step in finding an accountability partner is to compile a list of people who we already know might be a good fit, starting with our current circle of friends, family members, or coworkers. We should reach out to them, explain our goals briefly, and ask whether they would be keen to take on the challenge with us.

It would help to give any networking groups we belong to some consideration as well. Do we have any connections with somebody who we think may be a good match? We do not have to limit our quest to offline networking groups, of course, as we can also look for an online accountability partner. We can post information about our attempts in groups on Twitter or LinkedIn. A person who would love to collaborate with us might respond to our posts or message us privately.

LOOKING FOR VALUES THAT MATCH

We should think about our prospective accountability partner very carefully, choosing somebody whose values and viewpoints align with ours so that we can get the most out of our collaboration. For instance, you want to open up a new business. If you place a high value on servicing customers, and your partner cares more about earnings at the expense of clients, your relationship will not work. If your values clash with theirs, you won't be able to support each other. You need to research that person's background and credentials before agreeing to enter into an accountability relationship with them. Check their posts on social media, blogs, and websites. Do they frequently voice complaints about their clients? Do they regularly spread negative stories? When their name appears in your news stream, do you feel uncomfortable? All of these red flags should tell you that you will not get along with this person. When we are tempted to compromise our values and morals, a trustworthy accountability partner can be a big help.

KEEPING IT SHORT-TERM

We should keep things casual in the beginning when we discover somebody who we believe would be a suitable accountability partner. We should agree to a short trial period of between one to three months. Following this period, we can review our partnership and determine whether to keep it going. This allows us and our partners the chance to discuss our basic values, objectives, and principles. We must take our time and not rush our first meeting with our accountability partners because getting to know them can be exciting.

KEY TAKEAWAYS

- An accountability partner is a great addition to our accountability journey because they can offer guidance and advice, help us stay on track, and push our limits, while also sharing in our happiness and success.
- We have to also keep in mind that we need to be careful while choosing our accountability partners because the wrong person might seriously hinder our success while the right person can greatly help in achieving our goals.
- Things to pay attention to while choosing an accountability partner: They must be pursuing goals that match with yours, want responsibility for those goals as well, are at ease discussing sensitive information with you and you with them, and use similar methods of communication.

16

VISUALIZING YOUR SUCCESS

"Imagination is everything. It is the preview of life's coming attractions"- Albert Einstein

A lot of high achievers make effective use of the powers of visualization to plan, carry out, actualize, and accomplish their goals one small step at a time. While the rest of us may not be aware of or know how to use it, we all possess the power to visualize and achieve our goals. We benefit from visualizing because it allows us to establish important habits for success. Without it, we will not be able to continue moving toward our bigger life goals.

WHAT DOES VISUALIZING YOUR SUCCESS MEAN?

When we think about visualizing our success, we have two things in mind: visualization and success. So what exactly is visualization? It is the practice of constantly envisioning future goals as though they were already realized today. If we equate success with achieving these goals, then we can say that visualizing our success entails having vivid dreams and convincing our subconscious to embrace the way of life we associate with that success (Ngako, 2022). It is like giving ourselves the go-ahead to fulfill all of our lifelong goals and become whatever we ever wanted in life.

THE IMPORTANCE AND BENEFITS OF VISUALIZATION

We live in a world shaped by digital technologies that have opened new doors for business companies. Remote work is now accessible at the press of a button, but digital distractions often cause us to get sidetracked. Instead of trying to master multitasking, we need to take a step back and concentrate on the things that are most important to us. By utilizing the technique of visualization, we will be able to establish the mindset necessary to turn our future goals into reality.

In creative visualization, we can train our brains to concentrate on what is most important to us and to practice the process of selective attention. Have you ever purchased a car only to discover that everyone else appears to be using the same model? We see what we decide to pay attention to, and this is what selective attention means (Moe, 2021). Our chances of making a goal a reality increase the more we concentrate on it and work toward it.

By visualizing our success, we take control of our lives and ensure that it is in line with our long-term goals. The process also allows us to develop our ideas and see what is achievable. Additionally, visualization helps us remain aware of who we are as people and our life goals. Life becomes easier when we envisage our future as our present reality. Now that we understand why visualizing our success is important, let's take a closer look at the specific benefits we can reap from it.

INCREASING POSITIVE THOUGHTS

During the day, we will have a constant internal dialogue. Here, we need to be friends with ourselves and not destructive opponents, so we have to be conscious of our thoughts and pick them wisely. For example, if you are currently looking for a job, instead of thinking that you will fail and be unemployed forever, you need to visualize how you get a job and actually do the job in your mind. We will start attracting great results into our lives by thinking more positively today. The first day will not give us any noticeable changes, but reinforcement works like planting seeds. We will start to feel happier right away, and as time passes, things in our lives will start to change for the better.

DEFINING WHAT YOU WANT

By visualizing our success, we will be able to learn to shift our focus from what we do not want to what we do want to accomplish. We can let go of all the negative emotions and focus instead on the actions that will help us reach our own goals. For instance, if your goal is to buy a new car by this year, instead of thinking that you will not be able to save enough money, you should visualize yourself driving that car you want. In this way, you will be sure of what you want and then take the necessary steps in order to achieve that. Once your goal has been defined, you can then keep doing regular visualization exercises. The more specific our visualization, the more attainable our goals will seem to us.

IMPROVING MOTIVATION

Motivational visualization includes visualizing achieving our ultimate success and the emotions that go along with it. All our senses should be stimulated, and we should become so involved in a mental image that it feels real to us. For example, if your goal is to pass all of your exams, you can visualize it in your mind as if you have accomplished it. In this way, you will feel more motivated to study more in order to achieve this goal because you feel excited about the success that will come up in the future. The more you are accustomed to feeling successful, the more motivated you will be to complete your task, and the more likely you will be to succeed.

TIPS ON VISUALIZING YOUR SUCCESS

THINKING ABOUT YOURSELF GETTING WHAT YOU WANT IN LIFE

We can start off by focusing on the positive and allowing ourselves to believe that we will achieve our goals. It seems obvious, but the truth is that if we think we cannot do something, we will never succeed. Self-doubts can set us up for failure, but visualization helps to dispel them, thus fostering a growth mindset. That is all there is to it: visualizing ourselves achieving our objectives.

For example, we can picture ourselves taking a giant step to cross a fictional finish line or shaking the CEO's hands. The idea is to imprint that image in our minds. Then, it will be much easier to cultivate a positive attitude and feel confident in our ability to succeed. Nothing can stop us if we learn to visualize our success as if it has already happened. In addition, not even procrastination, which frequently interferes with our goals, can stop us here. To visualize achieving our goals is to affirm our commitment to them.

MAKING A VISION BOARD

The tip above concentrates on traditional methods of visualization through which a situation is internally visualized. However, some people have aphantasia, which prevents them from making up mental images (Ngako, 2022). We can alternatively make a vision board if we fall into this category or like to work with things that are concrete. Simply put, a vision board is a compilation of pictures and images that serve as a constant reminder of our own goals. Keeping a visual board somewhere close to your workspace will ensure that we stay on track—and true to our vision.

For example, if you want to lose weight, you can make a vision board with pictures of the things you wish to accomplish over time. You should not place your vision board too far away from where you can frequently view it. As a note, anything that can be measured can be monitored and improved upon.

PICTURING A HAPPY PLACE

Success may *look* different to different people, but it evokes the same feeling of contentment that you experience when you are, whether literally or metaphorically, in a happy place. When you struggle to finish a project and feel exhausted or overwhelmed, it helps to go to your happy place—a beach, an art exhibit, a rock concert, or anywhere you can unwind or recharge your batteries. Once you feel calm and relaxed, that place becomes a state of mind that you long to experience again and again.

EXPLORING POSSIBLE SOLUTIONS

In most instances, it is beneficial to think back on our visualization methods as a way of preparing for situations that might arise in the future. If the situation is uncertain or unpleasant, we can use this strategy. A good illustration is when we prepare to sit down with our supervisors and have a challenging discussion with them. If we plan ahead and visualize them, we will be aware of potential conversation topics and questions our supervisors might bring up. When we explore potential outcomes, the result frequently works in our favor. Furthermore, anticipating a possible problem allows us to better handle it as it occurs.

PLACING YOURSELF IN ANOTHER PERSON'S SHOES

There is a good chance that we can think of someone who, in the past, faced a similar obstacle to the one we are presently experiencing. We can imagine ourselves in their position right now. By doing so, we will be able to relate to the person's best or worst traits. When faced with an issue, we will come up with potential solutions to it. In order to visualize our success, it is essential to put ourselves in the other person's shoes. In that scenario, we should select a role model we admire and research the steps they took to achieve their success.

CREATING A NOTECARD

A notecard is a fantastic tool for detailing our success goals, keeping us in check, and reminding us of our daily tasks and long-term goals. Articulating our goals with conviction and intention can bring us closer to making them a reality. For instance, instead of something like, "My goal is to get a job as a software engineer by applying to various job vacancies," we need to be more specific: "I will get a new job as a software engineer by taking courses to improve skills in software development, creating a great resume, and then applying to good companies that are looking for a new software engineer." The clearer our intentions, the more inclined we will be to act upon them. Like the vision board, a notecard should be kept in a visible place, close at hand, so that we can refer to it frequently.

ADDING POSITIVE ENERGY TO YOUR VISUALIZATION

When we are feeling down, positive thinking can lift our spirits and lower our stress levels. Thus, we must think positively whenever we build our visualizations. Any negative thoughts we have should be met—so that they can be ultimately offset—by an equal amount of positive ones. We should avoid telling ourselves, "This goal seems too impossible to reach; I will never be able to accomplish it," for instance, and instead train our minds to reject these self-doubts with the belief that no matter the challenges we might face along the way, we can still succeed if we keep trying. A dose of optimism, however small, is all we need to start exploring the power of positive thinking.

KEY TAKEAWAYS

- High achievers frequently employ visualization strategies to accomplish their goals and achieve success.
- By visualizing our success, we will develop a positive attitude, motivate ourselves better, and clarify what we desire. Doing so will allow us to confront the obstacles that come our way head-on and overcome them.
- Some tips on visualizing your success: imagining yourself getting what you want in life, making a vision board, picturing a happy place, exploring possible solutions, placing yourself in another person's shoes, creating a notecard, and adding positive energy to your visualization.
- Naturally, visualizing our success becomes easier the more we practice it. That being said, the moment to begin practicing it is now.

17

FINDING YOUR WHY AND FOCUSING ON IT AS OFTEN AS POSSIBLE

"When something is important enough, you do it even if the odds are not in your favor."- Elon Musk

If we want to have consistent self-discipline, we would have to find real reasons and purposes for doing what we need to do. If we have ever had to deal with a serious crisis in our lives, we will have experienced the power of purpose to draw on energies, persistence, and bravery we probably were not even aware we possessed. Our mission was very clear and compelling. We had a laser-like focus. Our potential was also tapped. When we have a clear sense of purpose, we will be able to concentrate our efforts on the things that matter most, which drives us to take chances and move forward in spite of difficulties or challenges.

Imagine, for example, that you are attending a business meeting, or a school event when you receive a call that a member of your family has been severely injured in an accident and taken to the hospital. You will feel the urgent, desperate need to reach out to your loved one. Nothing else would concern you. Nobody and nothing could get in your way as you rushed to see your loved one. You'd be committed to doing whatever it takes for a strong reason. Thus, if getting there was the only challenge because you did not own a car, you might decide to run or perhaps even carjack one in order to go see your family member. If, when you arrived at the hospital, a security guard tried to stop you, would you give in and leave? Of course not. You would not act that way. You would do anything to enter the hospital room where your loved one was in.

Our lack of strong reasons for going after what we desire to accomplish is the root of all the excuses and foolish things we say and do that slow us back. In order to get what we desire we must be desperate. If we are not, we will fall into the 'I will like this or that" category of individuals who never get to experience the satisfaction of accomplishing their goals because they are not hungry or desperate for them. They lack compelling reasons to accomplish their life goals.

THE ADVANTAGES OF FINDING YOUR WHY

Humans have more desires in life than their animal counterparts, who are just motivated by the need to survive. We might experience discouragement, distraction, and hopelessness if we do not have an answer to the question, "survival for the purpose of what?" (Warrell, 2013). Understanding your why is a crucial first step in finding out how to accomplish the goals that motivate you and build a life you enjoy living rather than one you are just trying to survive. In fact, you will not have the ability to take the risks necessary to develop in life, keep going when things get tough, or radically change your life's trajectory until you first understand why you are doing what you are doing.

People who are aware of their life's purpose typically lead more fulfilling lives than those who are not. Because we are aware of who we are, where we have come from, and where we are going, we tend to live our day to the fullest. What, then, are some other advantages of knowing your why?

First, it gives meaning to our life. Once we know it, we will be able to get closer to our goals with each step we take and every bit of effort we put forth. When actions are taken with a clear purpose and objective in mind, they become significantly easier to complete.

Second, it establishes a value system. Knowing our why also enables us to identify and establish a set of basic values that will direct us in the years to come. For example, if you know that your purpose in life is to become a famous actor in Hollywood, you will focus on reaching it and taking the necessary steps in order to accomplish it. You do not have to waste time and effort every day attempting to determine whether what you are doing is actually right or worthwhile. You will know that you are on the right path if it fits your purpose. That greatly boosts your confidence in your actions.

Third, it boosts your self-esteem. We will have a great deal of pride in what we accomplish when we find our why and are striving toward something important. Our self-worth and sense of value will also grow with every day that goes by and with each little move we take in the right direction. We should use that feeling to motivate ourselves to face the obstacles that may arise in the future.

Lastly, it helps to improve your health, both physical and mental. Living a purpose-driven life can prevent depression and reduce the risk of stroke and cardiovascular disease (Willis, 2022). Indeed, finding meaning and purpose in our daily activities is one of the best methods to combat anxiety and stress (Morin, 2022).

TIPS ON FINDING YOUR WHY
KNOWING WHAT MAKES YOU FEEL ALIVE

We feel more alive when we are working toward goals that inspire us. These have to do with more than going on our dream vacation or watching our favorite football team play and win their game. As such, these goals reflect a deeper why, one that connects us with others and attaches us to something that is greater than ourselves. When we follow our passion, we focus on things that ignite that passion, but real fulfillment comes from the impact we have and the difference we make in the world around us.

We do not need to say right now that we wish to create the next Apple product, find a solution to the world's energy issues, or find a cure for cancer. Although we might in the future, this is about us getting involved with a cause that is both greater than ourselves and consistent with our values.

FIGURING OUT YOUR NATURAL TALENT

What are the things you have always excelled at and occasionally question why others find them so difficult? In the middle of complexity, are you able to spot patterns and potentials? Are you naturally inclined at thinking outside the box and being creative? Are you particularly skilled at completing tasks with such accuracy that other people find it boring? Are you great at details? Or are you an exceptionally talented networker, organizer, critical thinker, technologist, negotiator, or agent of change? Of course, we can also be skilled at something we do not feel particularly passionate about. However, as I have learned through experience, we rarely aim for goals that we lack the natural talent to accomplish.

ASKING FOR FEEDBACK

Oftentimes it might be challenging to identify the things we are enthusiastic and passionate about. After all, we likely have a wide range of interests, and it is possible that some of them have become so ingrained in our lives that we are unaware of their significance. Luckily, someone else may be able to provide some light on the situation. Without ever realizing it, there is a strong chance that we are already sharing our passions and purposes with the people around us.

We can decide to reach out to people and discover what they think of us or whom we remind them of. If someone compliments us or makes a comment about us, we should also try to pay attention to it. We can write down these observations and look for patterns in them. Whether others describe us as brilliant entertainers or admire us for assisting the elderly, hearing what these people think of us may reaffirm to us the passions we have already been pursuing.

ENGAGING IN CONVERSATIONS WITH NEW PEOPLE

While waiting for a friend at a restaurant or while riding public transportation by ourselves, it is very easy to turn to our smartphones and explore social media. We should try to suppress that urge and instead spend some time interacting with those around us. We can try to find out what they enjoy doing for entertainment or if they are working on any tasks. We can also ask them about any groups they are a part of or if they have a favorite charity they prefer to donate to.

Although starting to talk to individuals outside of our personal social circles might feel unpleasant at first, doing so can open our eyes to pursuits, issues, or employment opportunities that we were previously unaware of. Through this, we may be able to come upon unique activities to pursue or new destinations to explore, which will further assist us in discovering our why.

TURNING YOUR SUFFERING INTO PURPOSE

We all have our struggles and face different obstacles in life. When attempting to deal with a significant life change, a lot of people seek assistance from others. Some people later discover their calling by guiding those going through the same difficulties they did. Some people decide to work with and help people directly, as social workers, for instance. Other people choose to influence the lives of others through creating art and making music. Some others become life coaches, motivational speakers, or teachers to inspire others to better their lives and those of future generations. It is really up to us how we want to turn our suffering into something positive.

SUPPORTING A CAUSE YOU CARE ABOUT

A lot of people care about issues related to local, national, or global injustices and want to find solutions to them. What worries or bothers you in the world today? What do you feel strongly about? If solving problems like economic inequality, animal cruelty, racial and gender violence, global warming, or the mental health crisis is too daunting, remember that there are other causes out there—and organizations devoted to them—that could use our support. If the thought of elderly people spending the holidays by themselves makes us sad, or if we believe that drug users need more chances for recovery, then our purpose should be clear. As long as the cause is dear to our hearts, we can provide time, cash, or both.

SETTING ASIDE TIME FOR SELF-CARE

Self-care can take many different forms, and only we can define what that means for ourselves. Maybe we enjoy taking walks in the woods, practicing breathing techniques, or expressing our feelings in a journal. Why is self-care so crucial to practice? Because our minds are most productive and creative when they are comfortable and calm. When we compete with ourselves, we will never be able to accomplish anything or be of service to others. Have you ever realized that when you are showering, you discover a lot of great ideas? This is because when we let ideas come to us naturally rather than forcing them, our minds are more flexible and attentive to them. When our minds are relaxed, we instinctively think in creative ways, which can help us find our why.

KEY TAKEAWAYS

- Every successful person knows why they do what they do and have strong reasons behind it.
- Until we can find our why, we will continue living our lives on autopilot. We can get thrown off track, lost, and unsure of how to proceed or which way is forward. Even if everything is going well, we might still reflect on the past and wish we had used our time in a different way.
- Finding your why helps give your life meaning, establish a value system, boost your self-esteem, and improve your health.
- Tips on finding your why: knowing what makes you feel alive, figuring out your natural talent, asking for feedback from others, engaging in conversations with new people, turning your suffering into purpose, supporting a cause you care about, and setting aside time for self-care.
- Knowing your why gives you an internal compass that directs all of your choices and takes you on journeys that will enlighten your spirit.

18

BELIEVING IN YOURSELF

"To be a champ you have to believe in yourself when no one else will."- Sugar Ray Robinson

S ome believe that success is the result of wealth, luck, or relationships. While these and various other factors do affect each person's journey, success depends on our ability to believe in ourselves. Self-belief is key to self-confidence, which puts us on the path to success and, together with self-discipline, helps us stay strong in the face of adversities. When we allow self-doubts to take over, we become our own worst enemy. By the end of this chapter, you will learn both how self-belief can benefit you and how to develop it so that you can become your own biggest supporter in your pursuit of success.

THE ADVANTAGES OF BELIEVING IN YOURSELF

The key to both personal and professional success is self-belief. When you screw up and make a mistake, do you belittle yourself? Do you believe that speaking negatively to yourself will improve you in some way? Making a mistake is one thing, but eventually, we have to accept our mistakes and move forward. Otherwise, we will just be held back by that negative energy. We will not be able to take chances or do what is necessary to get toward our future goals. In the end, we must believe and have confidence in ourselves. We will be one step closer to creating a better life if we do this. Here are some advantages that we can consider in order to believe in ourselves.

YOU ARE THE ONLY ONE WHO CAN DO IT FOR YOURSELF

If we do not think that we will succeed and achieve what we want to do, how on earth would anyone else believe in us? Imagine you want to start a company and have to persuade the investors that your proposal is sound and worth investing in. If you don't truly think that your idea will work, nobody else will have faith in it. As another example, try to picture yourself with no arms or legs. This is the life that Nick Vujicic has to go through (Cama, 2022). At first he doubted his ability to lead a regular life and even tried to commit suicide. However, the turning point came when he started to believe in himself. Now that he is free of these limitations, Nick travels the world and tries to encourage millions of others to have faith in themselves no matter what.

To be sure, having a network of individuals who care about and support us will help a lot, but in the end, only we have the power to seize the opportunities that come our way. We need to have self-belief in order to thrive, and not merely survive in this world.

YOU MOTIVATE YOURSELF TO ACT

Once we can actually picture ourselves crossing the finish line, we become more driven to work toward our goals. We will keep trying until we succeed because we know it is possible and within our grasp. Consider the example of Michael Jordan, one of the most successful NBA players of all time. He has admitted that he had lost hundreds of games and missed thousands of shots before he became famous, but he understood that failure was a necessary part of the process, a source of motivation for him to work even harder and thus the catalyst of his great achievement (Nowik, 2022). We all may benefit from taking a lesson from Michael Jordan's attitude. Just remember that we are only getting closer to success even when we keep failing during our journey.

YOU BANISH NEGATIVE THOUGHTS

We will start seeing positive outcomes once we start thinking positively instead of negatively. How often have you told yourself that you cannot do something? I used to do it far too frequently. Since our minds love to make excuses for things, it is quite simple to come up with an explanation that appears convincing. Positive thoughts and affirmations about ourselves fill our minds, leaving no room for negative ones. And even when these negative ideas occasionally show up, our confident attitude will easily defeat them. For example, if you have an upcoming job interview, you should not get drowned in negative thoughts by thinking that the interviewer will ask hard questions you cannot answer. However, you should prepare different questions which you know the answer to and believe that you will be able to pass the interview because you have prepared yourself for it.

YOU BOOST YOUR CONFIDENCE

If we do not possess enough confidence, the first time we encounter a challenge, we will snap like a twig. Whatever we wish to do in life, there will always be obstacles that cast doubt on our abilities. Holding out hope that we can and will get past them is the only way here. For instance, if you want to launch a new business idea, there will be obstacles that you have to face, such as people's judgments saying that it is a bad idea, the difficulty of finding investors, or even the issue of finding new employees. If you hold on to the belief that you will launch this business, you will be confident that you can solve all of these issues and get through them. This self-confidence comes from a strong internal belief in our own self and capabilities.

YOU MAKE PROGRESS TOWARD SUCCESS AND ACHIEVEMENT

There must be one goal that we have in mind for a while. We are aware of the steps necessary to get there and the successes that have been accomplished by others. Since the pathway is now clear, all that is required of us is the belief that we can succeed before we begin it. By cultivating that optimistic attitude, we will come to understand that the only things standing between us and our goals are time and effort. Our likelihood of achieving our goals significantly rises when we feel like we are getting closer to them.

COMMON CHALLENGES TO SELF-BELIEF

Self-talk that is positive is much easier to say than to do. We must be in charge of our emotions, thoughts, and behavior in order to achieve it. It can be challenging to rewire our brains to think positively instead of negatively. Three common challenges to having self-belief are as follows.

COMPARING YOURSELF TO OTHERS

The key here is perception. Even if we may not be doing great, we might see someone else succeeding. For example, if you have browsed through social media, whether Instagram or TikTok, you must have seen people show off their new sports car or vlog their vacation to a new country. These things may be your dreams as well, and you envy those who have achieved them, but keep in mind that most people share only certain things on social media, and they often are not willing to showcase their difficulties and struggles in life. As the saying goes, "Don't judge a book by its cover." Moreover, there will be time for us to be successful if we try our best and believe in our abilities. We have to stay optimistic and appreciate what we have, without comparing ourselves to others and envying them.

FEARING YOUR PAST

Some say that the past can haunt us, and there is actually some truth to it. Perhaps you had a difficult childhood growing up in a broken family, or you were in an unhealthy relationship with someone who was physically abusive toward you. Although some wounds never heal, you should not let the past define you and hold you back because there is more to you than your trauma. A mental health specialist can help you work through these issues and prevent them from impacting your present.

HAVING TOXIC RELATIONSHIPS

Do you have a partner or friend who constantly criticizes you? Perhaps you fear meeting a parent or a coworker because they often make you feel inferior. Humans are by nature social creatures, but not getting someone's approval can be damaging to your self-esteem. If you feel like you have these kinds of people in your life, it is best that you stay away from them as much as possible. Instead of hanging out with toxic people, seek out new people who can support you so that you will be able to believe in yourself more.

A GUIDE TO BELIEVING IN YOURSELF

Like any critical life skill, self-belief is not developed overnight, but instead requires a lot of time and effort to build through honest reflection, positive thinking, fulfilling relationships, and obviously lots of practice. The challenges we have to face along the way can make it difficult for us to believe in ourselves. In order to help improve our self-belief, here are some guidelines that we can follow.

TAKING COMPLIMENTS GRACEFULLY

It might be hard for people who have extremely low self-esteem to accept compliments. For example, if such a person does not like their appearance and receives compliments about it, they will believe the person complimenting them must be lying in order to be polite. We should focus more on building our confidence if we often respond to praises with sarcasm or by rolling our eyes. However, if we are unable to identify anything nice about ourselves, we can start with the aspects others have praised or complimented us on. We should try to accept the compliment and smile, whether we deem it sincere or not. If we express our gratitude to that person, we will both feel more at ease and happy about it.

HELPING OTHERS

Understanding that we are not struggling with a particular situation that other people are going through helps us appreciate our good fortune, while also motivating us to help those in need. It is deeply satisfying to know that our actions had an impact on someone who needed our assistance. Indeed, although helping others allows us to forget about our problems and shortcomings, it also instantly boosts our self-esteem by bringing our strengths into focus. Thus, the more opportunities we seize to assist, volunteer, mentor, or educate others, the stronger our self-belief becomes as a result.

DOING THINGS THAT YOU FEAR

You are completely mistaken if you think that those who believe in themselves have no fears, anxieties, and second thoughts. For some people, these fears do not become a limitation to their success but rather challenges to improve themselves in the future. The best strategy for conquering fear is to face it head-on instead of running from it, no matter what our fear is—whether public speaking, meeting new people, or negotiating for a raise. Every day, we can try to do something that we fear in order to acquire more power to believe in ourselves from these experiences.

CHANGING YOUR BODY LANGUAGE

Our attitude, body language, and responses to various situations all serve as indicators of how much we believe in ourselves and our levels of self-esteem. Simply modifying our motions and body language can help us to have more self-belief. If others see that we believe in what we do, we will feel more confident in ourselves. Naturally, we can begin with a smile, decent posture, and eye contact with the person we are talking to. Self-belief is reflected in a smile, as well as in high shoulders and a straight back (Belyh, 2019). When we smile, we make others feel more at ease around us, which is a terrific way to enhance our self-belief.

MOVING FORWARD AND NOT LOOKING BACK

In the course of our lives, there will be many situations when we are bound to feel depressed and like giving up. However, we should never listen to the voice in our heads that tells us to quit and causes us to begin doubting ourselves. We must stay strong and keep moving forward until we reach our destination; upon arrival, we will see just how stronger the belief in ourselves and our abilities has grown.

CREATING A LIST OF THINGS YOU ARE PROUD OF

If we are struggling to maintain our self-belief in the face of challenges, we can try making a list of all the things we are most proud of—and thankful for—in our lives, regardless of how trivial they may seem. Furthermore, we need to think of this list as a work-in-progress and constantly update it to reflect our growth mindset. When kept nearby, whether on our work desks or pinned on a wall in our office, the list can serve as a constant reminder of our accomplishments when the going gets too tough.

FEEDING YOUR MIND WITH POSITIVE THINGS

The law of attraction holds some truth to it, in that both the positive and negative energy we put out into the world will eventually come back to us (Perry, 2022). This means that our thinking affects how we engage with the outside world and how others interact with us. How we view ourselves and the world has a lot to do with what we feed our minds with.

For example, we can try to find material that uplifts and inspires us, whether it be through books, films, or social media. Our brains will gradually change their thinking patterns if we frequently read encouraging and inspiring content. We also need to avoid people with negative or cynical viewpoints. Even though it is necessary to be realistic and acknowledge the obstacles life throws in our path, cynicism kills our motivation and undermines our belief in the future, in other people, and ultimately, in ourselves (Perry, 2022).

KEY TAKEAWAYS

- Believing in ourselves is a critical life skill that we need to master. Everyone is special, full of potential, able to grow personally, and deserving of self-belief. If we want to achieve the things we want to do in life, we need to believe in ourselves first because if we won't do it, who will?
- Some benefits that self-belief can offer us: motivating us to act, banishing negative thoughts, boosting our confidence, and enabling our progress toward success and achievement.
- Some challenges to building self-belief: comparing ourselves to others, fearing our past, and having toxic relationships.
- Some strategies for developing self-belief: taking compliments gracefully, helping others in need, doing things that we fear, changing our body language, moving forward and not looking back, creating a list of things we are proud of, and feeding our minds with positive things.
- The power of self-belief lies within each one of us, so it's up to us to let it propel us to success!

CONCLUSION

Now that we have reached the end of the book, I hope that you enjoyed learning some helpful tips for developing consistent self-discipline and that you will put them to good use. Remember, though, that all the insights and strategies that were covered here are just the first step on your journey toward self-discipline, and the next step is taking action. No matter how many books you read, nothing will actually change unless you actively implement the great ideas they teach you.

That being said, you may find that only some of the suggestions and exercises for training your mental muscle presented in this book apply, or maybe appeal, to you. In other words, you should not expect to immediately start making changes in every area of your life. You can choose one or two skills you would like to strengthen, or areas in which you need to improve, then move on from there once you are pleased with the outcome. Not only will you have developed stronger self-discipline in the process, but the fresh energy that such discipline provides will also prime you for the next challenge.

For example, if you are concerned about your physical health and fitness, then this is what you should focus on: establishing better and healthier habits. After all, if your body is not healthy, you will not be able to accomplish anything else in life. In order to make this vital change, you will need to exercise self-discipline.

Now, the key to developing mental toughness and self-discipline is commitment to your goals and consistency in pursuing them no matter the challenges at hand. By staying the course and sticking to your habit in order to successfully meet long-term goals in one area of life, such as health and fitness, it will be easier to accomplish similar goals in other areas. As it is often said, success breeds success, so it's important that you first achieve a small measure of success before aiming higher.

In addition to defining self-discipline and explaining its benefits, this book details the steps to take, the skills to practice, and strategies to adopt in order to become more self-disciplined. These ideas are highlighted at the end of each chapter that invites you to set specific goals and discover your why, try to do something that sucks, let go of things that you cannot change, take responsibility for your life, practice delayed gratification, stop listening to the naysayers, find a mentor to guide you, as well as an accountability partner, visualize your success, and last, but not least, believe in yourself!

If you possess the drive to succeed but are unsure where to start, I hope you will pick up this book and find guidance and inspiration in it. And if you have already set out on your journey to success, but there comes a time when you feel lost or disheartened, use this book as a stepping stone to help you find your way and regain confidence in yourself and your abilities to turn your vision of success into reality.

Everything worthwhile in life takes effort and time. Only those who can demonstrate discipline, determination, and dedication will reap the benefits of reaching their goals.

REFERENCES

Abdou, A. (2022, October 20). *7 key differences between having a growth mindset versus a fixed mindset.* The Ladders. https://www.theladders.com/career-advice/7-key-differences-between-having-a-growth-mindset-versus-a-fixed-mindset

Ali, A. (2021, February 9). *5 ways to be more self-disciplined and achieve your goals.* LinkedIn. https://www.linkedin.com/pulse/5-ways-more-self-disciplined-achieve-your-goals-dr-adnan-ali/

Arrington, C. (2022, February 1). *7 keys to successfully mastering self-discipline. Candy* Arrington. https://candyarrington.com/7-keys-to-successfully-mastering-self-discipline/

Bastos, F. (2019, January 3). *Control what you can: how to focus your energy in the right places.* Mind Owl. https://mindowl.org/control-what-you-can-control/

Belyh, A. (2019, November 25). *The incredible power of believing in yourself.* Cleverism. https://www.cleverism.com/the-incredible-power-of-believing-in-yourself/

Benefits of an accountability partner in business. (2022). Christian Women's Corner. https://www.christianwomenscorner.com/accountability-partner.html

Bokhari, D. (2022). *The ultimate guide to developing self-discipline.* Dean Bokhari. https://www.deanbokhari.com/the-guide-to-developing-self-discipline/

Bradi, K. (2022). *7 ways to eliminate your excuses.* Lifehack. https://www.lifehack.org/articles/productivity/7-ways-eliminate-your-excuses.html

Braun, K. (2023, January 9). *How an accountability partner can help you succeed.* Clever Girl Finance. https://www.clevergirlfinance.com/blog/accountability-partner/

Cama, M. (2022, October 26). *A life without limbs: Nick Vujicic uses his story to inspire students across globe.* Eagle Nation Online. https://eaglenationonline.com/44285/features/a-life-without-limbs-nick-vujicic-uses-his-story-to-inspire-students-across-the-globe/

Canelas, F. (2021, July 11). *7 reasons why you should (really) plan your days.* (2021, July 11). Filipa Canelas. https://www.filipacanelas.com/blog/7-reasons-why-https://www.lifehack.org/articyou-should-plan-your-days

Casano, T. (2022, March 16). *10 ways to believe in yourself again.* Lifehack. https://www.lifehack.org/288536/10-ways-believe-yourself-again

Castrillon, C. (2020, march, 8). *How suzy batiz bootstrapped her way to a $240 million empire.* Forbes. https://www.forbes.com/sites/carolinecastrillon/2020/03/08/how-suzy-batiz-bootstrapped-her-way-to-a-240-million-empire/?sh=77eb9f785fea

Celes. (2022). *7 important reasons why you should set goals.* Personal Excellence. https://personalexcellence.co/blog/why-set-goals/

Clear, J. (2018). *Atomic habit summary.* James Clear. https://jamesclear.com/atomic-habits-summary

Clear, J. (2020). *Atomic habits – book summary notes/highlights.* Ali Abdaal. https://aliabdaal.com/book-notes/atomic-habits-summary/

Clear, J. (2022). *How to build a new habit: this is your strategy guide.* James Clear. https://jamesclear.com/habit-guide

Clements, R. (2022). *10 ways to ignore the naysayers and achieve your dreams.* Lifehack. https://www.lifehack.org/articles/productivity/10-ways-ignore-the-naysayers-and-achieve-your-dreams.html

Consequences of lack of discipline. (2020, July 15). The Ellegee. https://www.theellegee.com/blog/consequencese-of-lack-of-discipline

D'Angelo, M. (2022, August 6). *How to find a mentor.* Business News Daily. https://www.businessnewsdaily.com/6248-how-to-find-mentor.html

Davy, P. (2019, November 3). *Do something that sucks, every day.* Medium. https://medium.com/@paul_37208/do-something-that-sucks-every-day-abcfbdd43df2

Demers, J. (2022). *7 ways successful people spend their free time.* Inc. https://www.inc.com/jayson-demers/7-ways-successful-people-spend-their-free-time.html

Downey, L. (2022, June 19). *Mark Zuckerberg: Founder and CEO of Meta (formerly Facebook)*. Investopedia. https://www.investopedia.com/terms/m/mark-zuckerberg.asp

Finkelstein, D. (2020, June 30). *Why should you have an accountability partner*. LinkedIn. https://www.linkedin.com/pulse/why-should-you-have-accountability-partner-darren-finkelstein/

Finkelstein, D. (2022). *What are the benefits of an accountability partner?* Tick Those Boxes. https://tickthoseboxes.com.au/what-are-the-benefits-of-an-accountability-partner/#:~:text=They%20Provide%20Support%20And%20Advice,require%20more%20attention%20and%20focus.

Firsich, M. (2020, May 22). *Do something that sucks today*. LinkedIn. https://www.linkedin.com/pulse/do-something-sucks-today-michael-firsich/

5 easy ways to gain the self-discipline to reach your goals. (2017, October 25). Absolute Cycle Bangkok. http://absolutecyclebangkok.com/5-easy-ways-to-gain-self-discipline-to-reach-your-goals/

5 reasons to ignore naysayers and pave your own pathway to success. (2018, January 19). Forbes. https://www.forbes.com/sites/steveolenski/2018/01/19/5-reasons-to-ignore-naysayers-and-pave-your-own-pathway-to-success/?sh=7919f5681e87

5 things successful people do that others don't. (2016, May 24). American Express. https://www.americanexpress.com/en-us/business/trends-and-insights/articles/5-things-successful-people-do-that-others-dont/

Goeke, N. (2018, November 29). *Atomic habits summary.* Four Minute Books. https://fourminutebooks.com/atomic-habits-summary/#:~:text=1%2DSentence%2DSummary%3A%20Atomic,massive%2C%20positive%20change%20over%20time.

Griggs, U. (2022, May 30). *How to stop making excuses and start taking responsibility.* Lifehack. https://www.lifehack.org/articles/mentalstrength/how-to-stop-making-excuses-and-get-what-you-want.html

Herrity, J. (2022, July 2). *How do you set SMART goals? Definition and examples.* Indeed. https://www.indeed.com/career-advice/career-development/smart-goals

How to build healthy habits in your daily life. (2022). Parodontax. https://www.parodontax.com/amp/how-to-build-healthy-habits.html

How to focus on what you can control (and win more battles). (2021, November 16). Soulsalt. https://soulsalt.com/focus-on-what-you-can-control/

How to plan your day: Benefits and 8 tips for success. (2021, November 25). Indeed. https://www.indeed.com/career-advice/career-development/how-to-plan-your-day

How to take responsibility for your life. (2022). Live About. https://www.liveabout.com/how-to-take-responsibility-for-your-life-1919214

Imafidon, C. (2022). *15 small things successful people do every day.* Lifehack.

https://www.lifehack.org/articles/productivity/15-small-things-successful-people-every-day.html

Ivers, I. (2020, July 22). *7 practical ways to stop making excuses.* Ivy Ivers. https://ivyivers.com/feel-good/7-practical-tips-to-stop-making-excuses/

Khan, H. (2021, February 27). *Discipline will take you to places where motivation can`t.* linkedIn. https://www.linkedin.com/pulse/discipline-take-you-places-where-motivation-cant-hamza-khan/

Khurana, R. (2021, August 13). *Ignore the naysayers from your life.* LinkedIn. https://www.linkedin.com/pulse/ignore-naysayers-from-your-life-rupinder-khurana/

Krbechek, A & Tagle, A. (2022). *Motivation is an unreliable emotion.* Npr. https://www.npr.org/2019/10/25/773158390/how-to-find-a-mentor-and-make-it-work

Lack of self-discipline. (2021, December 10). Evolve Inc. https://evolveinc.io/self-improvement/self-discipline/lack-of-self-discipline/

Manson, M. (2022). *The responsibility/fault fallacy.* Mark Manson. https://markmanson.net/responsibility-fault-fallacy

McNaney, J. (2015, February 12). *5 benefits we can reap from the power of visualization immediately.* Huff Post. https://www.huffpost.com/entry/5-benefits-we-can-reap-fr_b_6672638

Moe, K. (2021, June 4). *5 visualization techniques to help you reach your goals.* Better Up. https://www.betterup.com/blog/visualization

Morin, A. (2022, December 26). *Tips for finding your purpose in life*. Very Well Mind. https://www.verywellmind.com/tips-for-finding-your-purpose-in-life-4164689

Murphy, A. (2021, April 22). *9 ways to take responsibility for your life*. Declutter the Mind. https://declutterthemind.com/blog/take-responsibility/

Navided, A. (2020, November 27). *Marshmallow test experiment and delayed gratification*. Simply Psychology. https://www.simplypsychology.org/marshmallow-test.html

Ngako, P. (2022, March 12). *10 tips for using visualization for success*. LinkedIn. https://www.linkedin.com/pulse/10-tips-using-visualization-success-patrick-ngako-cpa-1c/?trk=articles_directory

Nowik, O. (2022). *7 powerful reasons why you should believe in yourself*. Lifehack. https://www.lifehack.org/articles/communication/7-powerful-reasons-why-you-should-believe-yourself.html

Parincu, Z. (2022). *Self-discipline: Definition, tips, & how to develop it*. Berkeley Wellbeing Institute. https://www.berkeleywellbeing.com/self-discipline.html

Pate, D. (2019, April 1). *7 myths about discipline you need to stop believing*. Entrepreneur. https://www.entrepreneur.com/living/7-myths-about-discipline-you-need-to-stop-believing/331400

Patel, N. (2022). *How to find a mentor online*. Neil Patel. https://neilpatel.com/blog/find-mentor/

Perry, E. (2022). *How to walk the freeing path of believing in yourself.* Better Up. https://www.betterup.com/blog/how-to-believe-yourself

Phelps. B. (2022). *The importance of keeping promises to yourself: Part 1.* Upside Therapy. https://www.upsidertherapy.com/blog/the-importance-of-keeping-promises-to-yourself#:~:text=Each%20time%20we%20keep%20a,follow%20through%20on%20our%20commitments

Robbins, T. (2022). *Importance of delayed gratification.* Tony Robbins. https://www.tonyrobbins.com/achieve-lasting-weight-loss/delayed-gratification/

Robinson, J. *Motivation or discipline?* (2022, August 8). Nasdaq. https://www.nasdaq.com/articles/motivation-or-discipline

Roepe, L. (2022). *10 tips for finding a mentor-and making the relationship count.* themuse. https://www.themuse.com/advice/how-to-find-a-mentor

Sasson, R. (2022). What is self-discipline? Definitions and Meaning. Success Consciousness. https://www.successconsciousness.com/blog/inner-strength/what-is-self-discipline/

Satterfield, D. (2020, February 14). *Discipline comes from within you.* The Leader Maker. https://www.theleadermaker.com/discipline-comes-from-within-you/

Scherr, M. (2022, July 21). *Successful people do the things that unsuccessful people won't.* linkedIn. https://www.linkedin.com/pulse/successful-people-do-things-unsuccessful-wont-michele-cole-scherr-/?trk=pulse-article_more-articles_related-content-card

Self-discipline for students. (2022). UO People. https://www.uopeople.edu/blog/self-discipline-for-students/

Self-discipline. (2022). Mind Tools. https://www.mindtools.com/adjf7nz/self-discipline

Stop living on autopilot. (2022). Hack Spirit. https://hackspirit.com/taking-responsibility/

Successful people do what unsuccessful people are not willing to do. (2022). Quotespedia. https://www.quotespedia.org/authors/j/jim-rohn/successful-people-do-what-unsuccessful-people-are-not-willing-to-do-dont-wish-it-were-easier-wish-you-were-better-jim-rohn/

Susman, D. (2022, February 17). *How to face your fears.* Very Well Mind. https://www.verywellmind.com/healthy-ways-to-face-y our-fears-4165487

Taking in the risk in life: 5 steps for determining worthwhile risks and achieving your goals. (2022, April 27). Soul Salt. https://soulsalt.com/taking-a-risk-in-life/#:~:text=Taking%20risks%20can%20change%20you,and%20can%20do%20it%20again.

10 things successful people do every day. (2022). Keep Inspiring. https://www.keepinspiring.me/10-things-successful-people-do-every-day/

Thakur, V. (2019, September 16). *Top 10 benefits of discipline.* LinkedIn. https://www.linkedin.com/pulse/top-10-benefits-discipline-vipan-thakur/

The benefits of planning your day the night before instead of in the morning. (2022). Amazing Marvin. https://blog.amazingmarvin.com/6-benefits-of-planning-your-day-the-night-before-instead-of-in-the-morning/

The power of taking full responsibility for your life. (2022, March 22). Gregg Van Ourek. https://greggvanourek.com/full-responsibility/

The powerful ways to cultivate extreme self-discipline. (2022). Forbes. https://www.forbes.com/sites/brentgleeson/2020/08/25/8-powerful-ways-to-cultivate-extreme-self-discipline/?sh=74090db6182d

The reasons why mentorship is important for mentee and mentor. (2022, August 30). https://www.indeed.com/career-advice/career-development/why-is-a-mentor-important

Tony, T. (2022). *How to stop making excuses*. Tony Robbins. https://www.tonyrobbins.com/productivity-performance/how-to-stop-making-excuses/

Turner, C. (2016, July 27). *Is discipline a choice?* Meetatroam. https://meetatroam.com/2016/07/is-discipline-a-choice/

Understanding laser focus, how to develop it and boost your productivity. (2022). Student Lesson. https://studentlesson.com/what-is-laser-focus-and-how-can-you-develop-it/

Ward, M. (2016, November 16). *Warren Buffett's reading routine could make you smarter, science suggests*. CNBC. https://www.cnbc.com/2016/11/16/warren-buffettsreading-routine-could-make-you-smarter-suggests-science.html

Warrel, M. (2013m October 30). Do you know your why? 4 questions to tap the power of purpose. Forbes. https://www.forbes.com/sites/margiewarrell/2013/10/30/know-your-why-4-questions-to-tap-the-power-of-purpose/?sh=380fb87473ad

Waters, S. (2021, June, 23). *How delayed gratification changes the way you live and work.* Better Up. https://www.betterup.com/blog/delayed-gratification#:~:text=Delayed%20gratification%20is%20the%20ability,for%20what%20you%20truly%20want.

What are atomic habits, and why use them to create your L&D strategy. (2022). Iseazy. https://www.iseazy.com/blog/atomic-habits/#:~:text=Atomic%20habits%20are%20small%2C%20repetitive,changes%20in%20our%20everyday%20lives.

Willis, A. (2022). *5 benefits of finding your purpose.* They Call Me Blessed. https://www.theycallmeblessed.org/5-benefits-finding-your-purpose/

Wooll, M. (2021, October 19). *Start finding your purpose and unlock your best life.* Better Up. https://www.betterup.com/blog/finding-purpose

Write down five positive things from each day. (2022). No Panic. https://nopanic.org.uk/write-down-five-positive-things-from-each-day/

Yeti, S. (2021, August 4). *Consequences you would face if you lack self-discipline.* Success Yeti.

https://www.successyeti.com/happiness/consequences-you-would-face-if-you-lack-self-discipline/2021/08/04

Yetman, D. (2021, June 21). *Exposure therapy*. Healthline. https://www.healthline.com/health/exposure-therapy#definition

Zimmerman, B. J. & Kitsantas, A. (2014). Comparing students' self-discipline and self-regulation measures and their prediction of academic achievement. *Contemporary Education Psychology, 39*(2), 145–155.

www.ingramcontent.com/pod-product-compliance
Lightning Source LLC
Chambersburg PA
CBHW071145120626
46546CB00006B/2128